D1547504

The Political Writings
of JOHN KNOX

The Political
Writings
of JOHN KNOX

The First Blast of the Trumpet
against the Monstrous Regiment of Women
and Other Selected Works

Edited and with an introduction by
Marvin A. Breslow

Folger Books
WASHINGTON: THE FOLGER SHAKESPEARE LIBRARY
LONDON AND TORONTO: ASSOCIATED UNIVERSITY PRESSES

© 1985 by Associated University Presses, Inc.

Associated University Presses
440 Forsgate Drive
Cranbury, NJ 08512

Associated University Presses
25 Sicilian Avenue
London WC1A 2QH, England

Associated University Presses
2133 Royal Windsor Drive
Unit 1
Mississauga, Ontario
Canada L5J 1K5

The paper used in this publication meets the minimum requirements of the American National Standard for Permanence of Paper for Printed Library Materials Z39.48-1984.

Library of Congress Cataloging in Publication Data

Knox, John, 1505–1572.
  The political writings of John Knox.

  "Folger books."
  Includes bibliographies.
  Contents: The first blast of the trumpet against the monstrous regiment of women (1558)—Letter to the Regent of Scotland (1558)—Appellation to the nobility (1558)—[etc.]
  1. Reformed Church—Doctrines—Addresses, essays, lectures. 2. Church of Scotland—Doctrines—Addresses, essays, lectures. 3. Woman (Christian theology)—Addresses, essays, lectures. 4. Women heads of state—Addresses, essays, lectures. 5. Church and state—Great Britain—History—16th century—Sources. 6. Reformation—Great Britain—Sources. I. Breslow, Marvin A., 1936–II. Title.
  BX9421.K56 1985   285'.241   84-47549
  ISBN 0-918016-75-4 (alk. paper)

Printed in the United States of America

Contents

Preface

John Knox was little more than a name to me until I began to study him in Professor John McNeill's seminar at Harvard, and my interest lapsed until Dr. Louis B. Wright, late director of the Folger Shakespeare Library, urged me to prepare this edition. Other tasks and the patience of the Folger made it too easy to postpone completion, and I now find that my acknowledgments are, in sad part, a necrology. Virginia LaMar, late editor at the Folger, gave me kindly guidance, and the late Dr. Mary Rechenbach was helpful with some of Knox's references. Professor Joel Hurstfield, whose scholarship and joyousness are missed, gave me criticism and encouragement. I am grateful to Professor Arthur J. Bellinzoni for his patristic learning and for his friendship. I am most pleased to thank my friend and former student, Professor Lawrence N. Powell, for his assistance and for his patient impatience.

The primary reason for offering this edition of Knox's political works is the value of the writings themselves. Although Knox is not a giant of original political thought, his ideas, in the heat of bitter conflicts, helped to shape some of the political transformations that attended the Reformation. This edition, by modernizing spelling and punctuation and by providing notes in addition to Knox's, should make the political ideas of this important sixteenth-century religious reformer more accessible to the twentieth-century reader. To further that purpose the introduction provides both the historical setting in which Knox wrote and commentary on what he wrote.

7

Introduction

In sixteenth-century Europe, dynastic ties and the person of the monarch were matters of weight in the stance of states and the course of religion; the year 1558 was marked by sudden alterations that affected dynastic ambitions, the strength of states, and religious hopes. England and Scotland were diplomatic pawns on one flank of the match between Catholic Valois and Catholic Hapsburg. Mary Tudor was wife to Philip II, and her England was wed to a Spanish diplomacy that lost for England its last shred of empire in France. Mary Stuart, who had been in France for most of her young life, was in this year married to the Dauphin Francis; while in Scotland her mother, the French Mary of Guise, continued to exercise the regency and maintain the old French-Scottish alliance renewed in her daughter's marriage. But by November the death of Mary Tudor had raised her half-sister Elizabeth to the English throne; and however cautiously she moved at first, Elizabeth could not be other than Protestant. In Scotland stirrings among a nobility that had made a profession of rebellion meant that, although Mary and Francis might assume the style of king and queen of England, the strength of France even in Scotland could be doubted.

The changes effected or previewed in 1558 are visible only in retrospect. The participants may be pardoned that they could not foresee the future but could only see today and reflect on yesterday. To those who sought religious reformation, reflection on the recent past made 1558 a day-to-day struggle in which most of the world's powers were uncertain or hostile to the Reformation. To John Knox, 1558 was another year of day-to-day engagement in the cause of the Reformation, and it was the time when engagements past and present compelled him to see and to say that the reform of religion might require political changes in those states where uncertainty or hostility endangered the reformation of religion and the salvation of souls.

In 1558 the prospects for the seedling of religious reform were uncertain in Scotland, where the only constant had been rapid change that seldom altered anything except names. Where England had suffered the worst manifestations of aristocratic factionalism for only half a century, Scotland endured the same over a period of several centuries. Minorities and regencies encouraged the most notable characteristic of Scottish political life: aristocratic rivalries that were strong enough to contest for power but not strong enough to create or to maintain governance. Membership of the royal council was changed by battle, murder, and exile; Scottish monarchs were kidnapped so often that the experience might be viewed as an initiation ritual. Thus, when in 1542, James V turned his face to the wall and died, it was said, of shame for the defeat at Solway Moss, he left a foreign wife, an infant heiress, cadet claimants, and a quarrelsome nobility. In brief, he left the crown of Scotland essentially as he had found it and in many ways as his daughter would leave it.

But one aspect of Scottish life was changing, and this change eventually reshaped Scotland. The reformation of religion at first added another element of division, but in time it unified factions and made Scotland a nation. This reformation is difficult to assess: its aim may be viewed as changing men's outlooks, or cleansing institutions, or both. Certainly the institution of the Roman Church in Scotland was open to reform, and some clergymen— notably those led by Archbishop Hamilton—attempted by means of provincial councils, statutes, and episcopal visitations to check the corruptions that wealth, time, and man can work on any institution.[1] When, according to one estimate, the revenues of the church were in excess of £300,000 while revenues of the crown's lands came to only £17,500, the temptations that abetted corruption can be appreciated.[2] The 1487 Indult between James III and the papacy had facilitated the powers of royal appointment in the church so that by the mid-sixteenth century income from the ecclesiastical endowment provided for royal bastards and their bastards, infant abbots, and aristocratic lay commendators.[3] The arrangements, comfortable to the great families, provided minimally, if at all, for the cure of souls. Although Archbishop Hamilton made gestures toward institutional reforms, the archbishop, an illegitimate son of the Earl of Arran, also found places in the church for his own children.

If the leadership was less than exemplary, its efforts also were often ineffectual or tardy. A cleansed clergy could not have satisfied the Protestant reformers' doctrinal demands, but it would have offered a shield of strength instead of providing a target. From the late 1520s onward, clear indications exist of Protestant motions in Scotland; and although there are persecutions and some executions, even Knox's martyrology seems to point to sufficient protection, or perhaps laxity, to permit the preaching of the new faith and iconoclastic demonstrations against the old.[4] By the 1550s, when more vigorous attempts were made by the Roman Church to reform itself, the hour was already late.

A factious nobility and a weak church might constitute promising ground for reformers; but the crown, weakened by absence, could not be ignored. By 1558 the young queen had been in France for a decade, during which time her interests in Scotland were represented as ably as possible by her mother, Mary of Guise. Among the stormy crosscurrents of Scottish political life—made more treacherous, if possible, by the fact that the monarch was a child, female, and absent—Mary of Guise survived and preserved the Stuart crown for her daughter. The queen dowager demonstrated political skills worthy of her family and her adopted country. In 1554 she became regent, replacing Arran, head of the Hamiltons, and the heir to the throne. She filled many of the offices of state with reliable Frenchmen as she sought to keep Scotland allied to France. She was Catholic, but her religious policies were largely political. In late 1557, faced with both aristocratic opposition to an attack upon England in support of France and the Protestant demands of the Lords of the Congregation, Mary of Guise temporized successfully. She did not mount an attack against England but managed to secure even Protestant agreement to the marriage of her daughter to the Dauphin. That achieved, the regent moved more firmly against the religious unrest that had been stirring Scotland. The reformers who had experienced a period of leniency from the crown and some support from the aristocracy in the form of the Lords of the Congregation, in 1558 faced only persecution by the crown and uncertain succor from an aristocracy motivated as much by family ambitions (against Scottish rivals and the French-dominated government) as by an interest in the reformation of religion.

In England the eleven years since the death of the most willful

Tudor had been a time of religious uncertainty and even rebellion that went far to reveal that what King Henry had wrought no man could easily undo. For Henry VIII had succeeded in subordinating church to state and identifying the Tudor dynasty with the Englishman's desire for the stability of the state.

Mary Tudor, for all her fervor, restored England's allegiance to Rome by means of her headship of the state church; if such a position embarrassed her, she could gain comfort from the fact that such dynastic identification brought her to the throne of her father and brother and preserved her against the rebellions of men disaffected toward her and her religion. Although Mary's tenure was a mark of her father's success, the disaffections in her reign were evidence of the changes loosed in her brother's reign. To the articulate and the ambitious the brief years of Edward VI had been heady and hectic. Englishmen whose desires for religious reform had been suppressed under Henry found favorable hearing under the new government; those whose appetite for innovation and ambition for power had not been fully satisfied also found new opportunities and a champion in John Dudley, Duke of Northumberland. Political men who sought wealth in the ecclesiastical endowment pressed for religious reformation, while religious reformers allied with those in power in order to press reformation on a somewhat bewildered people.

The result had been five years of change in which Protestantism in England caught up with the royal reformation of the church in England. Ideas and programs that had been kept in fearful silence while Henry ruled were openly discussed in his son's reign. When Imperial victories endangered many centers of the Reformation, exiled Englishmen and important continental reformers fled to the safety of England, where they were welcomed. England gave them shelter; they in turn nourished the ferment of Reformation from influential places in Cambridge, Oxford, and London. Doctrine and ceremony were debated, compromised, and tried, but all of the experimentation depended on the goodwill of the government that ruled in the name of the boy who embodied the Tudor dynasty and royal headship.

English loyalty to the Tudor dynasty survived the frail Edward VI, and loyalty and luck thwarted the attempted usurpation by Northumberland that would have denied the royal headship to Mary. As England's first woman ruler, she faced rebellions and religious discontents with the Tudor will, if not the Tudor charm. If the prospect of her accession gave the reformers reason for anxiety, Mary's struggle to gain the throne gave her solid reasons to doubt their loyalty. Nevertheless, she acted with restraint where she might have responded with terror. Although the public expression of enthusiasm that welcomed her could be attributed to the natural optimism lavished on any new ruler, it may have meant that for most Englishmen avoidance of civil war was more immediate and more important than speculations on the new sovereign's religious inclinations. Public loyalty to the legitimacy she represented and admiration for the courage she demonstrated outweighed the fears of some and the treasons of a few.

Arrests were made of persons clearly involved in the attempt to deprive Mary of her throne, but a sharp change in the official religion had to await several kinds of negotiation. Within England this meant that what had been established with the consent of Parliament had to be changed with the assistance of Parliament. Outside of England a reunion with Rome necessitated personal and diplomatic negotiations with the Pope, Cardinal Pole, and Mary's cousin, the Emperor.

In the meantime those Englishmen who feared the new government because of their religious views had a choice: they could remain or leave. Many, of course, stayed and lived quietly through Mary's reign. But about eight hundred decided that the better part of discretion was discretion, and they went into exile, joining the continental reformers who had been expelled in the beginning of the reign. The government did not hinder the departure of the exiles, who, at best, were regarded as unreliable. Now it was the turn of Englishmen to seek shelter in the reformed cities; but as they found hospitality and their religious identities in a Strasburg, Geneva, Zurich, or Frankfurt, they also found themselves in conflict with each other. Life in exile intensified differences; yet it was life. In England their brethren, because of prominence or a refusal to be silent, gave witness to their faith in flames that burned into the English imagination. While their brethren tasted fire, those Englishmen abroad and alive tasted the bread of exile and prayed or cursed the tyranny of a woman's unnatural rule.

England and Scotland shared an island, a border, and a well-founded mutual distrust. The occasional English ambitions to fix the border somewhere beyond the Hebrides were not directed at building Scottish trust. On the other hand, whenever an English monarch tried to take exercise in France, the Scots, almost as a conditioned reflex, crossed the border and raided England. That diplomatic triangle was not essentially altered by the marriage of

Henry's sister Margaret to James IV; and when Henry sought to renew the bonds of dynasty by marrying his heir to his grandniece, the heiress of Scotland, the courtship ritual included the burning of a good part of lowland Scotland by the English army. If the Reformation came by means of England, too much history, too many deaths made acceptance difficult.

With the marriage of Mary Tudor to Philip of Spain in 1554, the diplomatic triangle became a quadrilateral: Spain with a somewhat reluctant England as ally, France with a French-governed and French-garrisoned Scotland as its ally. The Franco-Scottish tie, which had often at least appeared to serve both parties, now served only France as a means to thwart, not England, but Spain. The French occupation in support of a French queen regent and a French foreign policy would make England appear a lesser evil in Scottish eyes. Full realization of this alteration in Anglo-Scottish relations was not achieved until the early years of Elizabeth. Though of secondary interest to Hapsburg or to Valois, England and Scotland were of primary interest to themselves; and some saw them in remarkably similar positions: both were officially Catholic but contained significant minorities sympathetic to Protestantism; both were diplomatic satellites to greater powers; both had come to this situation as a result of their women rulers.

By 1558 John Knox had seen and experienced several changes in England, the turmoils of his native Scotland, the hardenings and clashes in Europe. Had Knox died in 1557, historians of the period might have listed him, offered a footnote, or decently buried him in a dissertation.[5] That he would eventually merit any recognition comes as a surprise, in light of his obscurity before 1546 when he swells a scene, carrying a sword rather than a spear. He had been born near Haddington where his family was dependent upon the Earls of Bothwell, and he had studied at St. Andrews. At the time he becomes important historically, he was probably thirty-three years old and was engaged as tutor to a laird's son. Thus more than half of Knox's life is clouded by historical obscurity. He said he had been deep in "the puddle of papistry" but offers little else about his life or opinions before he met George Wishart.[6]

The association with Wishart was Knox's entry into history: it introduced him to the cause of reform, and it also initiated him into the violence and disaster of Scottish political life. The families of his students were the same Ayreshire gentry who encouraged and protected the public preachings of Wishart. To what extent Wishart was aware of their ties to England and their conspiracy against the regent, it is impossible to know. He may have been useful, but he could not be used. When these men recoiled from public action, Wishart still continued to preach; and when he knew danger was imminent, he sent Knox away only hours before his capture by the Earl of Bothwell and Cardinal Beaton. The arrest was made on 16 January; on 1 March, Wishart suffered at the stake; on 29 May, a band of gentlemen entered Castle St. Andrews and murdered Cardinal Beaton. Revenge for Wishart, England's interest, political rivalry, are all in the mixture of motives that made a murder.

Knox did not witness either Wishart's execution or Beaton's assassination, but he came to know well the setting. The assassins, joined by families and friends and supplied by England, held Castle St. Andrews against the ineffectual armed might of a briefly united Scottish government. In the meantime Knox and his pupils moved from place to place until their fathers summoned him to bring them to the besieged castle. They arrived on 10 April 1547, and in this garrison community of self-exiles—the first of his many exile experiences—Knox entered into his vocation of preacher and controversialist. In those spring and summer months of 1547 much of Knox's career was foreshadowed: he was among rebels, whose religious interest was not unqualified; he was a supporter who became chief spokesman in debates with Catholics; he encouraged the defenders while reproving them for their sinful lives; and his first sermon with its text from Daniel, chapter 7, identified the papacy as the temporal manifestation of the spiritual corruption of Antichrist. But, as Knox was to experience frequently, the minions of Antichrist must have their day. By the end of July the intervention of a French fleet and artillery was sufficient even to make the Regent Arran effective, and Castle St. Andrews surrendered. The gentlemen were sent to French prisons; the others, including Knox, were put into the French galleys.

After more than a year and a half, Knox was released by the French. He had served in the French fleet sent to Scotland in 1548. He had been ill, and he had been pressed to partake of Catholic services; but he does not seem to have been mistreated. Nor was he isolated. Not only were there other Scots among the rowers, but Knox was able to communicate with those whose rank had merited a French prison. They wrote Knox to ask whether with conscience they should attempt an escape. His reply might be seen as a first enunciation on the questions of obedience and resistance. He told them "that if without the blood of any shed or spilt by them for their deliverance, they might set themselves at freedom." But he added that the prisoners should be assured that God would deliver them and they should not refuse his deliverance.[7] Knox was at this moment counseling nonviolent resistance to civil power, but, more than that, he was advocating obedience to God. The prisoners did escape without bloodshed, and a few months later they met John Knox in England.

In the England of Edward VI reformers in exile found more than simple shelter; they could find positions and rewards. For Knox, who was yet a small figure in comparison to a Peter Martyr Vermigli or a Martin Bucer, there was no Regius professorship—a position that would have ill-suited him as much as he would have ill-suited it. Instead, the place of preacher in the garrison town of Berwick was thought appropriate for him. It was, for there he could preach to and tend a congregation. The pastoral exercise was always his foremost concern. Although historically, his importance was political, it must be remembered that Knox was more concerned with rooting out the Roman Mass than overthrowing princes. That the one could not be accomplished without the other was his historical burden, but his interest and desire were in the cure of souls. In Berwick he was able to devote himself to that task. His pastoral zeal required that his congregation should not be led astray by idolatrous ceremonies. When his preaching attracted official attention, he began to move into a larger world than Berwick. In April 1550, in answer to a summons, he spoke against the Mass before an audience that included the conservative Bishop of Durham and other officials at Newcastle. By the end of the year Knox was made preacher at Newcastle, and within another year he was appointed one of the six royal chaplains.

The duties of his chaplaincy required him to leave Newcastle for a time and come to London in the autumn of 1552. There, at the center of change, were feverish scramblings and rivalries; the clashes of ideas, personalities, and powers. Edward was sickly, Somerset gone, and Northumberland and his gang were ascendant. Amid the babble of reformers and the growlings of conservatives, Archbishop Cranmer was pushed into further reformation, while at the same time trying to preserve some of the church's endowment from those who held political power. London provided fertile ground for a man of Knox's public talents, which were those of a preacher rather than a peacemaker. At the time of his arrival the second Book of Common Prayer was in the press. Although a clearly Protestant revision, it was the product of compromises. One such compromise enjoined the laity to kneel at communion. To Knox this was the old enemy—idolatry. Employing his place in the pulpit of the royal chapel, he attacked the ceremony as dangerous and joined with others who already had protested it. The royal council, in an effort to settle the dispute, asked for the opinions of the royal chaplains. The conclusion of the dispute was the addition to the Prayer Book of the "Black Rubric" which explained that kneeling was not to be understood as adoration. Although Knox, who won both praise and blame for the addition, was not fully satisfied, he accepted and urged conformity to the decision of the civil power.

Throughout his last year in England the pattern of controversy and conformity was repeated. Offered the bishopric of Rochester, he refused it. He returned to Newcastle where from the pulpit he sometimes denounced the corruptions of government, thereby attracting unfavorable attentions from those in power. Later, when offered a London vicarage, he refused that, too; but he did go south and, at the government's request, continue his preachings. Then and afterwards Knox was an enthusiastic admirer of the young king, but he apparently had grave doubts about Dudley and little appreciation of Cranmer. The area of opposition appears limited. To a zealous reformer such as Knox, men who were part of the government appeared either corrupt or confused; nonetheless, those same men supported the reformation of religion and protected it from the Catholic forces—Henrician or Roman—within England. To the men who wielded the powers of government during a royal minority, the zealous reformers could be a nuisance, but their efforts could be used to quicken religious support for a government whose serious opposition had a Catholic focus. The government could summon and admonish its Protestant critics, but it could not afford to persecute them. Knox could criticize the faults of governors and could quarrel about specific ceremonies, but the imperfections in church and state were not so overwhelming as to forbid conformity or to compel disobedience. So long as the government, motivated by whatever forces, was favorable to the reformers, there could be hope for improvement.

Hope was a dying boy-king. Knox delivered a sermon before Edward in April 1553, and he was preaching in Buckinghamshire when the king died in July. During the frantic days of Northumberland's attempted coup and Mary's eventually triumphant courage, Knox was a mere bystander. Throughout Mary's summer of toleration he was able to travel freely about England and to preach without hindrance.

It was a nervous season. By early autumn the continental exiles had departed England and renewed their wanderings. The new queen's first Parliament convened and began to return official religion to the practices used at the end of her father's reign. Fearful of enforcement, some reform-minded Englishmen prepared to follow the continental visitors. Scurrying about the country, settling his personal matters, John Knox also made his preparations for departure. In January of 1554 he landed at Dieppe; behind him Wyatt's rebellion gave Mary's government additional cause for hostility toward Protestants.

From January to July Knox journeyed through Switzerland, the vital center of the Reformation, returned to Dieppe, and again turned back to Geneva. Although he traveled throughout France and Switzerland, his mind was fixed on England. More precisely, his mind was fixed upon his friends in an England where the aftermath of Wyatt's rebellion, the trials of prominent clergymen, and the queen's announced intent to marry Philip of Spain, added to the afflictions of the reformed. To friends and former congregants Knox could not offer the consolation (consolation perhaps as much to him as to them) of preaching. Denied the pulpit, he employed the pen to bridge distance and to fulfill duty. But in offering written comfort to the afflicted, like any good pastor he was aware of the immediate situation of his readers and of the source of their danger. The impulse of his consolatory epistles was pastoral: he lamented, comforted, encouraged, admonished.

Although the impulse was pastoral, the circumstances that required him to write were political. His exile and the oppressions of his friends were the effects of a new ruler. The first of Knox's writings, "An Exposition Upon the Sixth Psalm of David," barely mentioned politics. He emphasized forbearance, the view that the present troubles were given by God who eventually would show his mercy.[8] In February he issued "A Godly Letter of Warning or Admonition to the Faithful in London, Newcastle, and Berwick," in which he announced the punishment of England for her lack of faith, her persecutions of the faithful, and her restoration of idolatry.[9] After the warnings, Knox offered some suggestions to the faithful: the faithful must not maintain idolatry nor teach it to their children; idolatry and idolaters must be destroyed. Then he asked, "Sall we go and slay all ydolateris?" Knox's reply to his own question was that drastic actions were the duty of the civil magistrates; the people only were required to avoid idolatry. Thus, Knox offered the Protestants a position of passive disobedience to their Catholic rulers, and he suggested that there were possible instruments of resistance.[10]

The pastor's political voice was stronger in May when he composed "An Epistle to his Afflicted Brethren in England." Assurance was given that God would preserve the faithful and take vengeance on the persecutors of the faithful. Forbearance was still a prominent theme: "Lat us pacientlie abyd with groyning and with sobbis, the tyme that is appoyntid to our correctiun." But something stronger was suggested: "But heirof be assureit that all is not lawfull nor just that is statute by Civill lawis, nether yet is everie thing syn befoir God, whilk ungodlie personis alledgeis to be treasone."[11] Knox hinted at a definition of "lawful" upon which a justification of resistance to authority could hinge, but it was still only a hint.

The hint was not developed further in July when he wrote "A Faithful Admonition to the Professors of God's Truth in England." Although one of Knox's better known tracts, it offered no new viewpoint: Mary Tudor and the English idolaters were a punishment to be suffered, for God would avenge the professed faithful. What was new was Knox's tone, for he introduced a cannonade of invective in which Bishop Bonner, Bishop Gardiner, Mary Tudor, her consort Philip, and Philip's father, the Emperor Charles V, were personally and viciously assaulted.[12] The pastor's political voice was stronger; it was learning to speak with a trumpet's stridency.

The vituperation of the "Admonition" armed Knox's opponents; not for the last time, the timing of his verbal blasts retarded his cause. When in the fall of 1554 he answered the call of the English congregation at Frankfurt, he rejoined the controversy over the form of worship prescribed in the Book of Common Prayer. It is not necessary here to recite the "Troubles at Frankfurt." For England the episode prefigured both the Elizabethan settlement and the divisions between moderates and Puritans. For Knox Frankfurt was a controversial way station on the road to reformation. He left after his adversaries showed an embarrassed city government his libels against the emperor. When he left Frankfurt, he took the road to Geneva.

From May to August of 1555, Knox rested in Geneva. In those months Geneva was in the last struggles that were to make it

Calvin's Geneva. Calvin had chided the Frankfurt congregation for its unbrotherly treatment of Knox, and Knox was apparently content to remain a quiet guest with the small English congregation in Geneva.[13] (A few years later, however, Calvin was discomfited politically by Knox's writings.)

Knox soon returned to Scotland, prompted perhaps by personal reasons; for with her father dead, Knox was able to wed Marjorie Bowes. But it was more than marriage that kept him in Scotland for the next eleven months. The political situation was fluid (as was typical of Scotland) and permitted the reformed preachers considerable freedom. The dowager queen regent was intent on maintaining her daughter's throne and securing the French alliance. The Roman Church was neutralized by weakness and by the coincidence that its leader in Scotland, Archbishop Hamilton, was of the family that stood as heirs and rivals to the young Stuart queen. The nobility were jealous of the French advisers who occupied offices of state and upon whom the regent relied. The political standoff that resulted inhibited the power to persecute the reformed preachers.

The reformed preachers used the political moment for their missionary work. The ground that had been seeded for a decade was cultivated with a zeal that assured future harvest. Foremost among the workers was Knox. In Edinburgh he was as surprised with his own popularity as he was pleased with the interest in his message. Great lords came to hear him and brought him to their seats in the country. From these vantages he denounced idolatry and demonstrated the celebration of the Lord's Supper. He was not, as he had been in England, a pastor of established congregations; he was a missionary, making converts, founding congregations, creating the future.

The permanent work was with the congregations, but the present and the near future were with the men who had invited Knox to return to Scotland. These were not the handful of assassins from the days of Castle St. Andrews; these were some of the most powerful lords in Scotland. Their interest in Knox and their power were demonstrated in May of 1556 when Knox was summoned before the bishops in Edinburgh. He answered the summons, but he was not alone: with him were some of his new friends and their men. The bishops withdrew the summons. The powers that could inhibit persecution could protect the preachers, could perhaps even foster the new faith.

The disinclination of the bishops to confront Knox and his protectors must have raised his spirits. Certainly his sights were raised, for he now addressed himself to the regent. Mary of Guise might have helped to dissuade the bishops from their prosecution of Knox; if so, this could account for the tone of moderation in his letter. He urged her to accept reformation, but he understood that "albeit suddenly ye may not do all things that ye would, yet shall ye not cease to do what ye may."[14] She could, he suggested, bridle the bishops, which would aid the preachers of reform, and she could study the religious issues for the good of her own salvation. Knox's concern for the soul of Mary of Guise was consonant with his pastoral mission: her soul was as valuable as any other. But the princely place of the regent evoked the prophet as well as the pastor in Knox. Were she to hearken to the truth he spoke, he could assure her a long life, temporal glory, and the succession of her posterity to the throne. In 1558 Knox republished this letter with lengthy additions that transformed it into one of his major political writings, but in 1556 the letter was the hopeful effort of one who, though calling himself "a worm most wretched," could address a queen regent in the style of a prophet.

Late in that summer John Knox, his wife, and mother-in-law traveled to Geneva. No certain explanation exists for his return at that moment. Affairs in Scotland seemed better for his cause than they had ever been, and he was not apprehensive of any danger. The only explanation he offered was that his "little flock" of Englishmen in Geneva had called him.[15] The call of one small congregation, not wanting for a preacher, seems insufficient compared to the reformation of a nation, but it must have weighed heavier on Knox's scale. Until the following spring, he enjoyed in Geneva the last peaceful interlude in his career; family and congregation filled his life.

But politics sought him. In May 1557, four Scottish noblemen wrote him, asking him to return. They told him that reform grew even as the friars fell in the estimation of the nobility and the regent.[16] With Calvin's assurance that this call was God's, Knox left for Dieppe, his usual port of transit. When he arrived on 24 October, he learned that he was not to continue to Scotland; the lords wanted a postponement. The war between France and Spain had reopened with Scotland and England as the sideshow. For the Scottish nobility the war provided an opportunity to bargain with the queen regent, and from their point of view it was not the time for Knox to appear and bring religious controversy to a head.

Neither for the first time, nor for the last time, John Knox discovered the unreliability of the Scottish nobility. His response this time was a letter that exploded with anger. He questioned their courage and their religious sincerity; he measured their political niceties against God's commands. For their failure Knox promised "grievous plagues and punishments" would befall "every inhabitant of that miserable realm and island." He especially warned the nobility "that thraldom and misery shall apprehend your own bodies, your children, subjects, and posterity, whom ye have betrayed."[17] That much was the angry prophet's denunciation. But near the end of the letter Knox introduced his own political note, one that he soon expounded as a major political theme: the nobility was an estate with divinely commanded rights and responsibilities, among which was the protection of religion and its professors. For the relief of the oppressed brethren "you ought to hazard your own lives (be it against kings or emperors) for their deliverance."[18] John Knox, the pastor of consolation, now joined with John Knox, the preacher of rebellion.

Knox remained at Dieppe for over two months before returning to Geneva. In Dieppe he was nearer Scotland, and Scotland was foremost in his mind. On 1 December, he wrote "To His Brethren in Scotland," a letter in which pastoral concern was the dominant tone. Addressed to the common people, the letter warned them against sectarian divisions and urged them to maintain a true church.[19] On 17 December, Knox again turned his attention to the politically powerful, to whom he wrote "To the Lords and Others Professing the Truth in Scotland." The anger evident in his previous letter to the nobility had passed, and the exhortation was moderated. Instead, he told them how necessary it was that they fear God, for without that fear their labors were vain. With the prophet's assurance of God's truth, Knox attempted to define their duty in negative terms: they must not "suddenly disobey or displease the established authority in things lawful," nor must they pervert their cause to assist in the ambitions of the Hamiltons. But then Knox tried to define what their lawful duty was: if possible, they should win the favor or at least the toleration of authority; failing to achieve the cooperation of authority, they must provide true preaching, true sacraments, and the defense of their brethren from persecution. Five times in the last two pages he urged lawful obedience to the civil authority, but everything else he demanded, in effect, reduced obedience to courtesy and restricted civil authority to property disputes. The tone was less passionate than in

October, but the message was more reasoned and, therefore, more dangerous.[20]

Not all of the anxious time at Dieppe was spent in waiting and in letter writing, for it was during his wait in Dieppe that Knox wrote *The First Blast of the Trumpet Against the Monstrous Regiment of Women.* Today the title invariably amuses history classes, and the title alone preserves Knox in one collection of famous quotations. In his day the work—not just the title—enlarged his fame, angered his opponents, and embarrassed his friends. Although Knox retracted nothing, the promised *Second Blast* was no more than a dwarfish couple of pages, and the final part of the trilogy was never born. His opinions remained the same, but the situation had changed.

Knox's thesis was that a woman ruler was unnatural—a monstrosity. Fundamental to his thesis was a conception of a knowable natural order in which natural and unnatural were distinguishable. God had created this ordering, making it visible to man's perceptions through laws and inspired instruments. In this hierarchical universe unnatural meant that something was not in its ordained place. Knox held this assumption in common with almost everyone else in his century. What he had to demonstrate was that a woman ruler violated the accepted universal order.

He began his demonstrations by insisting that one had only to use sight and reason in order to understand that the female was the inferior in nature. Female frailty made women inherently incapable of rule. History, with the exception of the Amazons, offered no example of women ruling men, and even among animals the female was subordinated to the male.[21] Knox also employed law, as it reflected nature and codified human reason, to show the inferior place of women. Roman law, which was more important to Scotland and the continent than to England, was cited by Knox. He interpreted the law as recognizing the weaknesses of women, and, therefore, imposing civil restrictions upon them.[22]

Both reason of nature and civil law were common to civilized man, and both were the legacy of gentile antiquity. Although the guidance of the ancients could be useful to his case, to Knox the revelation of divine ordinance outweighed all else.[23] God's commands, he claimed, made it a virtue for woman to serve man, and God's punishment of Eve made woman subject to man. For a woman to rule over men and for men to accept that rule were unnatural disorders, repugnant to God's law and, therefore, without legitimacy or justice.[24] Disobedience to law and subversion of order required divine vengeance for which Knox found biblical and contemporary examples.[25] If the Bible guided contemporary political life, he needed to explain some apparent exceptional cases—most notably, Deborah—in order to forestall critical objections. His response was that the exceptions were only that: God alone could exempt; man could not.[26] Against the explicit laws of God, it was vain for men to plead customary usage; they must, by opposing woman's tyrannical rule, obediently conform to God's order.[27]

Although Knox framed his arguments so as to enunciate a universal truth, his audience was England and Scotland more than it was Christendom, and in *The First Blast* it was England more than it was Scotland. Mary Stuart was a stranger to Scotland and her mother only regent; Mary Tudor, however, ruled England in such a way as to inspire and to confirm Knox's view of women rulers. Under this Jezebel, this Athaliah, the godly were persecuted, even slain, and England was led under a Spanish yoke to do the bidding of foreigners. When Knox tolled the names of Latimer, Ridley, Cranmer, and Lady Jane, he felt that these English martyrs proved to his age the effect of violating God's command against female rulers.[28] England suffered because its monarch was a woman, but the English monarch was a woman because England deserved Mary Tudor. As the criminal and the victim reflect and require each other, England's sins required punishment through a Mary Tudor, whose regal place was itself a sin: the sinner was punished by means of additional sin. Mary's restoration of the Roman Church and her persecutions of the Protestants were appropriate to England's failure to use fully the opportunities under Edward VI. Had England, as Knox and others had urged, removed all shreds of Romanism and wholeheartedly supported reform, then the grounds for the present afflictions would not have existed. Instead, corrupt and politic leaders had sought their own gains and had compromised the Church of God. Failing to grasp God's gift, England had turned away and had madly celebrated the accession of Mary whose unnatural rule now was England's punishment and humiliation.[29]

If England had accepted a full reformation under Edward, presumably Mary would not have become queen. England, half reformed, seemed to have had a choice between rejecting Mary or falling deeper into sin. Knox certainly could not propose that England should have raised either Lady Jane or Elizabeth to the throne, for they, of course, came under the sexual prohibition against women rulers; but he implied, without naming any candidate, that at Edward's death England might have chosen someone other than Mary. If this interpretation is correct then *The First Blast* attacked monarchy from two directions.

His main attack was negative: a woman ruler exercised power illegally. God's commandment overrode all human laws and customs. The unique, perhaps sacred, character of royal inheritance was insufficient justification for a woman ruler when weighed against divine prohibition. By denying exemption to monarchy, Knox left monarchy a little less exalted.

His other attack contained an implicitly positive element. When he denounced England's acceptance of Mary, who was a punishment England had earned, he was suggesting that somehow the monarch was a matter of choice. If England should not have accepted Mary, it seems to follow that England need not have accepted her. Perhaps this implication contained no more than a vestige of the coronation formulas, but whatever was behind it, the idea offered some alternative to a mystery embodied in a particular family's bloodlines (this view seems to have a parallel in the denial by Knox and most of the reformers that a priestly caste controlled the mystery of the sacraments). Although directed against the unnatural and illegal rule of women, *The First Blast* indirectly sounded against the order of kings.

Knox did not lack clarity when he attacked women rulers, but he was less clear when he advised what to do about them. In *The First Blast*, the nobility of England and Scotland specifically were criticized for having become "slaves of Satan and servants of iniquity."[30] They were told not only that they must seek God's forgiveness but that henceforth they must not serve their unnatural mistresses. Knox then stated that the nobility—the classic lower magistracy—could withdraw their allegiance and could remove the usurper from her office. He cited biblical examples, though these either demonstrated God's nomination of a leader to head a rebellion or showed God requiring defeats (as in the case of Wyatt's rebellion) before permitting victory.[31] In conclusion, *The First Blast* said that if the nobility rebelled against the sinful, illegal, and unnatural rule of women, the rebellion would be successful because God would have chosen the leader and the moment for the success. Knox told men what they must not do; he did not clearly tell them what they must do.

The First Blast was intended to call men to action, and Knox must have known that it would also summon his enemies. What he could not have foreseen was that his message, and especially the timing of his message, would compel disavowal by some friends and would create opponents of potential allies.

With the almost simultaneous publication of Christopher Goodman's *How Superior Powers ought to be Obeyed,* many reformers, particularly those associated with Calvin, feared to be identified with attacks on monarchy just as a generation earlier Luther had shunned identification with the peasant revolts. The accession of Elizabeth in November made Knox an embarrassment, if not a danger, to the reformers and their efforts, and their apologies generally followed the conciliatory line of thinking that Bullinger had outlined. Whether or not Knox regretted the discomfort he had given his friends, his letters show that he felt he had acted out of conscience and could not have acted otherwise.[32]

The first attempt at a full answer to Knox was written from exile by John Aylmer, later bishop of London. *An Harborrowe for Faithfull & Trewe Subiectes* was somewhat unusual in that it addressed the issues and avoided personal attacks almost entirely, seeking "not fo muche to reprove hym, as to proue the matter and fatiffie tender myndes."[33] One method Aylmer used was to heap up historical examples of women rulers.[34] His purpose, however, was not to argue the equality of women in governance. What his examples and arguments demonstrated was the omnipotence of God, a sign of whose strength was the employment of the weaker vessel in the greatest of tasks.[35] Aylmer also developed the thesis that was to become a bulwark of Elizabethan Anglicanism: Scripture teaches obedience; it does not prescribe polity.[36] The application of this thesis was that English laws and institutions permitted a woman sovereign, and it would be ungodly, unlawful, and un-English for subjects to be other than obedient to their queen.[37]

With the important exception of his justification of English custom, Aylmer's thinking is not remarkably different from Knox's. Whether a woman ruler was considered monstrous or a special sign of God's power, she was outside of the normal order. In the specific case of Elizabeth, Knox and Aylmer were largely in agreement: she had been preserved by God in order to restore Protestantism in England; should she do otherwise, her right to rule was doubtful. Aylmer's words were softer than Knox's rude ones, but the message was the same.[38]

In many ways *The First Blast* was an unfortunate distraction. Although bitter in tone, Knox's arguments are not any more antifeminist about the role of women in government than the arguments offered in defense of that exceptional role. From this perspective Knox's thoughts are fairly typical of the sixteenth century. From the perspective of his pastoral work, as his letters seem to suggest, he had a higher regard for the abilities of women than did many of his contemporaries.[39]

The First Blast was also an unfortunate distortion; for although it fits with Knox's writings on the right of disobedience, its notoriety eclipsed his other more considered political works of 1558. *Letter to the Regent of Scotland, Appellation to the Nobility,* and *Letter to the Commonalty of Scotland* were published in Geneva where Knox had returned from Dieppe by way of La Rochelle and Lyons. Where *The First Blast* aimed at England, albeit Knox's interest was universal, the three letters that followed were addressed to his native Scotland. Each of the traditional orders— ruler, lower magistracy, and commons—received specific attention, and with the act of publication the entire nation was informed of its errors and its duties.

Letter to the Regent of Scotland announced the immediate cause behind all three works: Scotland owed a duty to God and to Knox to correct the error of the Scottish bishops when they had passed a sentence of excommunication against Knox. In 1556, when Knox, accompanied by armed supporters, had answered the summons of the ecclesiastical court, the bishops had backed down. However, during his absence in Europe, they had judged him and had sentenced him. At the time of the original summons Knox had written to Mary of Guise. In a tone that was moderate and even hopeful, he had exhorted her to reform religion. After the sentence against him, he republished that first letter, but his additional commentaries were harsh and admonitory.

Admonishing the prince was a prophet's task, and the additions of 1558 emphasized that role. The prophet as corrector could not respect rank, for his authority was the highest. Again and again Knox cited the Old Testament examples of prophets judging kings and of differences in rank cast aside by God's commands.[40] Knox, as prophet, also explicitly pointed out the biblical parallel to Scotland and its royal family. The deaths of the queen regent's two sons and husband were a punishment on her and on James V. The survival of a daughter marked the end of the Stuart dynasty; for Scotland the inheritance was the curse of a woman as ruler.[41]

Letter to the Regent of Scotland was a prophet's warning to the prince, but it also was the condemned man's appeal to the magistrate. In both undertakings Knox appeared to perform a prescribed exercise, a legal requirement: the prophet must warn and warn a second time; the condemned man must appeal to the legally responsible officer. To Mary of Guise Knox now had fulfilled his duties as a prophet of the Reformation and as a subject of Scotland.

Letter to the Regent of Scotland echoed *The First Blast*'s note that a woman ruler was a curse. Perhaps more important was its implicit dismissal of reliance upon princes. The summer of 1558 was not the season to be hopeful of either princely reform or justice, for almost all monarchs appeared arrayed and armed against the Reformation.[42] Knox, therefore, aimed beyond the monarch, at the subject, and subjects again were told that they must not obey the inferior law of the state when it was contrary to the superior law of God. He did not elaborate, but he promised to write other letters on the powers and responsibilities of the nobility and of the people.[43] To the crown's representative he had made his formal appeal and his prophetic warning; hence, he could take his case and God's cause to the nobility and to the people.

Knox's *Appellation to the Nobility of Scotland* was the most important of his political writings. By addressing his appeal to the Scottish nobility, he recognized their role in Scotland's history; by providing them with religious reasons for political action, he assisted the course of Scotland's future. *Appellation* articulated political ideas that in Knox's earlier writings had found only partial or tentative expression. In Protestant political thought, *Appellation* stands as the most effective, important Calvinist statement on political resistance to be made between Calvin's earlier, hesitant hints and later, vigorous Huguenot arguments on resistance.

Appellation first must be seen as an appeal, for its larger message was argued within a legal framework. Within that framework Knox could claim that, having exhausted all other appropriate steps without securing justice, he had to take the next step: not a simple appeal of the episcopal sentence from the prince to the nobles; it was instead, as it had been in *Letter to the Regent of Scotland*, an appeal to "a lawful and general council" that could decide the religious controversies.[44] The likelihood of the meeting of such a council was less than small, but Knox made the formal acknowledgment that also maintained a recognition of an authoritative body in Christendom. Until a general council spoke for Christendom, his legal appeal was limited to Scotland.

Although *Appellation* was addressed to the nobility of Scotland, the appeal went beyond one nation's boundaries or a specific moment in history. Whether in Scotland or Judea, all knowledgeable men were bound to God's commandments. Responsibilities for the enforcement of those commandments were not, however, the same for all men. God had provided each man with a vocation—a place in life—and in broad terms the different vocations had different responsibilities. They all were bound to God, but Knox also held that they were all also bound to each other. In Knox's view, each vocation is linked to the others and each is linked to God. He does not see them in the traditional hierarchical arrangement: linked to God through each other. Instead, Knox's view is that God created princes, nobles, and commons; each, according to its vocation, is directly responsible to God. Each vocation also has responsibilities to the other vocations: princes have duties to nobles and to commons; nobles have duties to princes and to commons; commons have duties to princes and to nobles.[45]

Developing from that significant alteration of the traditional hierarchical arrangement, this appeal forcefully presented the responsibilities of the Scottish nobility. They were reminded that they were as other men except for their offices, and those offices were put upon them by God. Knox did not explicitly deny the hereditary principle, but, as in *The First Blast*, his emphasis on the offices of the lower magistracy could be read as a diminution of heredity in nobility. Nobility as an office was ordained by God; individuals who happened to occupy those places had to employ those offices in accordance with God's rules.

To employ those offices in accord with God's rules meant that the civil magistrate bore a responsibility for the practice of religion. Civil office was empowered to protect and to punish, and for Knox this power included an obligation to protect the people by punishing the bishops. This obligation required more than the negative punitive power, for it also necessitated positive actions. The magistrate was responsible for providing the common people with good religious guidance. Knox dismissed the excuse that religious matters were the exclusive domain of the clergy when he cited biblical and historical cases to show that God had commanded the civil magistrates to correct ecclesiastical wrongs and to support the practice of true religion.[46]

Knox's arguments for the religious responsibilities of the civil power were no innovation in the political thought of Europe, where the realization of that idea was as near to Scotland as the England of Henry VIII. What was innovative in *Appellation* was the application to the lower magistracy of this idea of the religious responsibilities of the civil power, for in thought and in political reality this idea usually was applied to the higher magistracy, the prince. Knox was concerned with when and how these responsibilities fell to the lower magistracy, the nobility. They were, he claimed, a group with religious obligations that were the same as the prince's. When the prince persecuted true religion or supported false religion, the nobility was bound to uphold God's commandments and to check the prince. Knox acknowledged that God commanded obedience to the prince, but, as he illustrated from the Old Testament, this obedience did not extend to the prince who would subvert true religion or destroy its believers. Should the nobility fail to undertake the duties owed to God and to the people, then, Knox assured them, they would suffer divine punishment.[47]

No longer was passivity to be the stance of the persecuted. By raising the collective lower magistracy to the level of the prince, Knox could assert that the nobility must act even against the prince in the support of religion and the suppression of idolatry. He went so far as to allow that it would be legitimate action if only some of the nobility took up their swords.[48] For Scotland, *Appellation* was a call to arms, appealing to those who had the arms, and it was a justification for rebellion to those Scottish nobles who had a tradition of rebellion. It had, in addition, a less parochial appeal; for wherever the monarch stood opposed to reformation, another part of the political order was under a religious imperative to undertake reformation at the point of the sword. In 1558, the application of this imperative could have been almost everywhere in Western Christendom.

In *Appellation* Knox invoked the protection of religion by the nobility on the ground that protection was a responsibility attached to their vocation. In *Appellation* he also stated that everyone had some kind of divinely ordered vocation and that each vocation had some responsibility for religion. In *Letter to the Commonalty of Scotland*, which was published at the same time as *Appellation*, Knox appeared more clearly in his vocation of preacher as he attempted to instruct the common people of Scotland in their religious responsibilities and their rights.

The instruction he offered was in part a simplified rehearsal of the arguments he had used in the other tracts. Again, he emphasized that religion was not the exclusive preserve of the clergy but that it must be the paramount interest of each and of all. The truth of religion was not to be found in either antiquity or customary acceptance but must, instead, be tested against Scripture.[49] Knox made these familiar points in a manner that differs from that in the other tracts; in *Letter to the Commonalty* the language and its rhythms appear more colloquial, less formal, less harsh than in the other works. When he wrote for his "dearly beloved brethren," he wrote as a pastor among his flock.

Knox invited this flock, this common congregation of Scotland, to witness his appeal. They were not to be judges between him and the bishops, for the place of judges was that of the nobility. They were, however, to attend as audience to the contest between Roman priests and Protestant preachers. From this debate they would hear how the priests had deceived them, and they would learn what God expected of them.[50] This invitation recreated Knox's first public role when he had been tutor, pastor, and disputant in Castle St. Andrews. St. Andrews was magnified into Scotland, and John Knox now was prepared to offer political guidance to his enlarged congregation.

Knox's political guidance presumed lines of obligation among the three parts of the kingdom. He informed the commonalty that one obligation of princes and nobles was to provide for religion. Should they fail such provision or should they uphold false religion, the commonalty were not absolved of their own responsibilities to God. Having heard the truth of religion, the commonalty must be obedient to God, and obedience meant maintaining true religion despite the failure of the magistrates. Two actions were allowable: they could provide for their own preachers, and they could withhold their dues from the priests.[51] Neither action constituted a right of rebellion in the same way that rebellion was permitted to the lower magistracy against the prince, but the independent provision of preachers by the commonalty clearly represented more than passive resistance.

The ground for Knox's political guidance of course was religion. He did not even hint that the commonalty could withdraw from any other duties owed to superiors, and certainly the removal or punishment of errant superiors was not in their hands. But religion, as it concerned the salvation of each soul, was a measure of equality between rulers and subjects. Greater responsibilities attended the greater offices of rulers, but even the lowliest subject, once informed of the truth, could not avoid his own direct religious responsibilities. To avoid divine punishment required abstention from idolatry and withdrawal of support from the priests, but to demonstrate obedience to God by supporting true preachers required limited resistance to the magistrate. The equality of souls had entered the political world.

A reading of Knox's political tracts of 1558 provides a picture of the victorious prophet. In part this picture can be drawn from Knox's aggressive tone. He was not the appellant on the defensive; he was on the attack in style and in argument. All of the tracts contain examples of divine punishment against the persecutors of true religion and the maintainers of false religion. All of the tracts predict divine punishment for those contemporaries who supported idolatry or suppressed Protestantism. This style of decrying sin and foretelling wrath was a strong element of the prophetic tradition; and when Knox wrapped himself in that tradition, he appeared self-assured, free from doubts.

That picture of Knox the victorious prophet is a part of these writings, but it also can disguise much that is essential to Knox and to these works. The 1558 tracts, like the earlier political writings, were composed in a dark time. Mary Tudor in England and the French control of Scotland were the realities of the moment, and no one could have foretold that within months Elizabeth would reign in England and soon thereafter assist in expelling the French from Scotland. That was the unpredictable, unlikely future. For Knox, the desperate and needful present required pastoral explanation and exhortation. Denied the pulpit, Knox used the printing press to address the larger congregations of England and Scotland. He took his particular case and turned it into a larger cause that attempted to provide guidance in a dark time.

His tone was aggressive, his message strong, but desperation lent strength and also provided clarity. Since the days of Castle St. Andrews and his sentence in the French galleys, Knox had been compelled to consider questions of persecution and resistance. Gradually, events had sharpened his thought so that he had moved from acceptance and consolation through passive resistance to rebellion. He had moved from a position where persecution could be understood as a sign and a test of religious conviction to the position that proclaimed that the threshhold of suffering had been passed. True religion, having been tested for its truth, now had to be defended.

In the defense of religion Knox summoned each of the traditional orders of society. Certainly Knox is not original in his concept of a three-part order, but what is notable is not only his emphasis that each part is ordained by God but that each part has particular responsibilities to each other part as well as to God. Thus, kings are responsible for their rule and the conduct of that rule, but kings also are responsible to the other parts of society. The commonalty owe obedience to nobles and to the king, but the commonaltys' responsibility to God for their own religious practices transcends the ladder of obedience to nobles and to kings. In the sixteenth and seventeeth centuries when issues of religious practices touched almost everything else in political life, this doctrine of Knox's provided a formidable weapon for rebellion, if not for revolution.

For Scotland, Knox's religious justification for political rebellion suited the normally rebellious Scottish nobility well, and with Elizabeth's aid they expelled the French and allowed the establishment of Protestantism. Later, with Knox's encouragement, some of the nobility defeated and deposed Mary Stuart. Although Knox often was disillusioned by the Scottish nobility's lack of religious commitment, he and they had served each other well: he had provided religious grounds for their rebellions; their rebellions opened fields for the planting of his church.[52]

Within that church, which became rooted among the Scots and grew to be exemplary for many English, the obligation to defend religion was not lost. In limiting and then deposing Mary Stuart, the nobility had Knox's exhortation to destroy idolatry as a religious justification for their rebellion. In defending their church, Scots and then English discovered religious justification for the revolution that defeated, tried, and in 1649 executed Mary Stuart's grandson, Charles I.

Notes

1. Gordon Donaldson, *The Scottish Reformation* (Cambridge, 1960), 33–46.

2. Gordon Donaldson, *Accounts of the Collectors of Thirds of the Benefices, 1561–1572* (Edinburgh, 1949), xv.

3. Matthew Mahoney, "The Scottish Hierarchy, 1513–1565," in *Essays on the Scottish Reformation*, ed. David McRoberts (Glasgow, 1962), 44.

4. John Knox, *History of the Reformation in Scotland*, ed. W. C. Dickinson (New York, 1950), vol. 1, 11–74 *passim*.

5. Jasper Ridley, *John Knox* (Oxford, 1968) is the best scholarly biography of Knox, and I have followed it for the information on Knox's life. The most recent biography is W. Stanford Reid, *Trumpeter of God* (New York, 1974), but it is no replacement for Ridley. Some interesting insights can be found in the more popular biographies, Edwin Muir, *John Knox: Portrait of a Calvinist* (New York, 1929) and Lord Eustace Percy, *John Knox* (London, 1937).

6. In the modern edition of Knox's *History of the Reformation in Scotland* Knox does not mention himself until p. 67.

7. Knox, *History*, vol. 1, 109.

8. John Knox, *The Works of John Knox*, ed. David Laing (Edinburgh, 1846–64), vol. 3, 119–56.

9. Ibid., vol. 3, 165–215.

10. Ibid., vol. 3, 194.

11. Ibid., vol. 3, 235–36.

12. Ibid., vol. 3, 257–330.

13. Ibid., vol. 4, 59.

14. Ibid., vol. 4, 83.

15. Knox, *History*, vol. 1, 123–24.

16. Ibid., vol. 1, 132.

17. Ibid., vol. 1, 134.

18. Ibid., vol. 1, 135.

19. Knox, *Works*, vol. 4, 261–75.

20. Ibid., vol. 4, 276–86.

21. See pp. 43, 57–58.

22. See pp. 44–45.

23. See p. 45.

24. See pp. 45–64 *passim.*

25. See pp. 58–60, 63–64.

26. See pp. 65–73.

27. See pp. 73–78.

28. See pp. 58–60, 77–78.

29. See pp. 57–60, 66–67, 77–78.

30. See pp. 59–60.

31. See pp. 74–77.

32. Knox, *Works*, vol. 5, 5–6; vol. 6, 76–77; *The Zurich Letters*, ed. Hastings Robinson (Cambridge, 1846), 76–77; R. Dareste, "Hotman d'après de nouvelles lettres des années 1558–1561," *Revue historique* 1 (1876): 20.

33. John Aylmer, *An Harborrowe for Faithfull & Trewe Subiectes agaynst the late blowne Blaste concerning the Gouvernmet of Women, wherein be confuted all such reasons as a stranger of late made in that behalfe* (Strasburg, 1559), sig. C2.

34. Ibid., sig. C3–F4v.

35. Ibid., sig. B2–B3, I1–I1v, M1v–M2v.

36. Ibid., sig. G1v–G4.

37. Ibid., sig. H3–H3v, K4–L2v.

38. Ibid., sig. N1–O4v; Knox, *Works*, vol. 6, 47–51.

39. Knox, *Works*, vol. 3, 331–402; vol. 4, 217–53, *passim.*

40. See pp. 89, 94–95, 98–101.

41. See pp. 96–98.

42. See pp. 83–84.

43. See pp. 87–89, 91.

44. See pp. 81–82, 105–6.

45. See pp. 116–17, 129–34.

46. See pp. 116–19, 135–40.

47. See pp. 124–35.

48. See pp. 134–35.

49. See pp. 148–49.

50. See pp. 147–48, 154–55.

51. See pp. 155–56.

52. Knox, *History*, vol. 2, 13–20, 82–84, where Knox confronts Mary Stuart with the arguments of his political tracts.

The Political Writings
of JOHN KNOX

1

The First Blast of the Trumpet Against the Monstrous Regiment of Women (1558)

Preface

The Kingdom appertains to our God.

Wonder it is that amongst so many pregnant wits as the isle of Great Britain hath produced, so many godly and zealous preachers as England did sometime nourish, and amongst so many learned and men of grave judgment as this day by Jezebel are exiled, none is found so stout of courage, so faithful to God, nor loving to their native country, that they dare admonish the inhabitants of that isle how abominable before God is the empire or rule of a wicked woman, yea, of a traitoress and bastard. And what may a people or nation, left destitute of a lawful head, do by the authority of God's word in electing and appointing common rulers and magistrates? That isle, alas, for the contempt and horrible abuse of God's mercies offered, and for the shameful revolting to Satan from Christ Jesus and from his Gospel ones professed, doth justly merit to be left in the hands of their own counsel and so to come to confusion and bondage of strangers. But yet I fear that this universal negligence of such as sometimes were esteemed watchmen shall rather aggravate our former ingratitude than excuse this our universal and ungodly silence in so weighty a matter. We see our country set forth for a prey to foreign nations; we hear the blood of our

37

brethren, the members of Christ Jesus, most cruelly to be shed; and the monstrous empire of a cruel woman (the secret counsel of God excepted) we know to be the only occasion of these miseries; and yet with silence we pass the time as though the matter did nothing appertain to us. But the contrary examples of the ancient prophets move me to doubt of this our fact. For Israel did universally decline from God by embracing idolatry under Jeroboam. In which they did continue even unto the destruction of their commonwealth.[1] And Judah with Jerusalem did follow the vile superstition and open iniquity of Samaria.[2] But yet ceased not the prophets of God to admonish the one and the other, yea, even after that God had poured forth his plagues upon them. For Jeremiah did write to the captives in Babylon and did correct their errors, plainly instructing them who did remain in the midst of that idolatrous nation.[3] Ezekiel from the midst of his brethren prisoners in Chaldea did write his vision to those that were in Jerusalem, and, sharply rebuking their vices, assured them that they should not escape the vengeance of God by reason of their abominations committed.[4]

The same prophets for comfort of the afflicted and chosen saints of God, who did lie hid amongst the reprobate of that age (as commonly doth the corn amongst the chaff), did prophesy and before speak the changes of kingdoms, the punishments of tyrants, and the vengeance which God would execute upon the oppressors of his people.[5] The same did Daniel and the rest of the prophets, every one in their season. By whose examples and by the plain precept, which is given to Ezekiel, commanding him that he shall say to the wicked: "Thou shalt die the death."[6]

We in this our miserable age are bound to admonish the world and the tyrants thereof of their sudden destruction, to assure them, and to cry unto them, whether they list to hear or not, that "the blood of the saints, which by them is shed, continually cries and craves vengeance in the presence of the Lord of hosts."[7] And, further, it is our duty to open the truth, revealed unto us, unto the ignorant and blind world, unless that to our own condemnation we list to wrap up and hide the talent committed to our charge. I am assured that God hath revealed to some in this our age that it is more than a monster in nature that a woman shall reign and have empire above man. And yet with us all there is such silence as if God therewith were nothing offended.

The natural man, enemy to God, shall find, I know, many causes why no such doctrine ought to be published in these our dangerous days. First, for that it may seem to tend to sedition. Secondarily, it shall be dangerous not only to the writer or publisher but also to all such as shall read the writings or favor this truth spoken. And last, it shall not amend the chief offenders, partly because it shall never come to their ears and partly because they will not be admonished in such cases.

I answer, if any of these be a sufficient reason that a truth known shall be concealed, then were the ancient prophets of God very fools who did not better provide for their own quietness than to hazard their lives for rebuking of vices and for the opening of such crimes as were not known to the world. And Christ Jesus did injury to his Apostles, commanding them to preach repentance and remission of sins in his name to every realm and nation. And Paul did not understand his own liberty when he cried, "Woe be to me, if I preach not the Evangel."[8] If fear, I say, of slander or of any inconvenience beforenamed might have excused and discharged the servants of God from plainly rebuking the sins of the world, just cause had every one of them to have ceased from their office. For suddenly their doctrine was accused by terms of sedition, of new learning, and of treason.[9] Persecution and vehement trouble did shortly come upon the professors with the preachers; kings, princes and worldly rulers did conspire against God and against his anointed, Christ Jesus.[10] But what? Did any of these move the prophets and Apostles to faint in their vocation? No. But by the resistance which the devil made to them by his supposts[11] were they the more inflamed to publish the truth revealed unto them and to witness with their blood that grievous condemnation and God's heavy vengeance should follow the proud contempt of grace offered. The fidelity, bold courage, and constancy of those that are passed before us ought to provoke us to follow their footsteps, unless we look for another kingdom than Christ hath promised to such as persevere in profession of his name to the end.

If any think that the empire of women is not of such importance that for the suppressing of the same any man is bound to hazard his life, I answer that to suppress it is in the hand of God alone; but to utter the impiety and abomination of the same, I say, it is the duty of every true messenger of God to whom the truth is revealed in that behalf. For the especial duty of God's messengers is to preach repentance, to admonish the offenders of their offenses, and to say to the wicked, "Thou shalt die the death, except thou repent." This, I trust, will no man deny to be the proper office of all God's messengers, to preach, as I have said, repentance and remission of sins. But neither of both can be done except the conscience of the offenders be accused and convicted of transgression. For how shall any man repent not knowing wherein he hath offended? And where no repentance is found, there can be no entry to grace. And, therefore, I say that of necessity it is that this monstriferous empire of women (which amongst all enormities that this day do abound upon the face of the whole earth is most detestable and damnable) be openly revealed and plainly declared to the world to the end that some may repent and be saved. And thus far to the first sort.

To such as think that it will be long before such doctrine come to the ears of the chief offenders, I answer that the verity of God is of that nature that at one time or at other it will purchase to itself audience. It is an odor and smell that cannot be suppressed; yea, it is a trumpet that will sound in despite of the adversary. It will compel the very enemies to their own confusion to testify and bear witness of it. For I find that the prophecy and preaching of Elisha was declared in the hall of the King of Syria by the servants and flatterers of the same wicked king, making mention that Elisha declared to the King of Israel whatsoever the said King of Syria spoke in his most secret chamber.[12] And the wondrous works of Jesus Christ were notified to Herod, not in any great praise or commendation of his doctrine, but rather to signify that Christ called that tyrant a fox, and that he did no more regard his authority than did John the Baptist, whom Herod before had beheaded for the liberty of his tongue.[13] But whether the bearers of the rumor and tiding were favorers of Christ or flatterers of the tyrant, certain it is that the fame, as well of Christ's doctrines as of his works, came to the ears of Herod. Even so may the sound of our weak trumpet by the support of some wind (blow it from the south or blow it from the north, it is no matter) come to the ears of the chief offenders. But whether it do or not, yet dare we not cease to blow as God will give us strength.[14] For we are debtors to more than to princes, to wit, to the multitude of our brethren, of whom, no doubt, a great number have heretofore offended by error and ignorance, giving their suffrages, consent, and help to establish women in their kingdoms and empires, not understanding how abominable, odious, and detestable is all such usurped authority in the presence of God. And therefore must the truth be plainly spoken that the simple and rude multitude may be admonished.

And as concerning the danger which may hereof ensue, I am not altogether so brutish and insensible but that I have laid mine account what the finishing of the work may cost me for mine own part. First, I am not ignorant how difficult and dangerous it is to speak against the common error, especially when that the ambitious minds of men and women are called to the obedience of God's simple commandment. For to the most part of men, lawful and godly appeareth whatsoever antiquity hath received. And secondarily, I look to have mine adversaries, not only of the ignorant multitude, but also of the wise, politic, and quiet spirits of this world; so that as well shall such as ought to maintain the truth and verity of God become enemies to me in this case as shall the princes and ambitious persons, who to maintain their unjust tyranny do always study to suppress the same. And thus I am most certainly persuaded that my labor shall not escape reprehension of many.

But because I remember that accounts of the talents received must be made to him, who neither respects the multitude, neither yet approveth the wisdom, policy, peace nor antiquity concluding or determining anything against his eternal will revealed to us in his most blessed word, I am compelled to cover mine eyes and shut up mine ears, that I neither see the multitude that shall withstand me in this matter, neither that I shall hear the opprobries nor consider the dangers which I may incur for uttering the same. I shall be called foolish, curious, despiteful, and a sower of sedition; and one day, perchance, although now I be nameless, I may be attainted of treason.

But seeing that impossible it is but that either I shall offend God, daily calling to my conscience that I ought to manifest the verity known, or else that I shall displease the world for doing the same, I have determined to obey God, notwithstanding that the world shall rage thereat. I know that the world offended, by God's permission, may kill the body; but God's majesty offended hath power to punish body and soul forever. His majesty is offended when that his precepts are contemned and his threatenings esteemed to be of none effect. And amongst his manifold precepts given to his prophets and amongst his threatenings, none is more vehement than is that which is pronounced to Ezekiel in these words: "Son of man, I have appointed thee a watchman to the house of Israel, that thou shouldst hear from my mouth the word, and that thou mayest admonish them plainly, when I shall say to wicked man: O wicked, thou shalt assuredly die. Then if thou shalt not speak, that you mayest plainly admonish him, that he may leave his wicked way, the wicked man shall die in his iniquity, but his blood will I require of thy hand. But and if thou shalt plainly admonish the wicked man, and yet he shall not turn from his way, such a one shall die in his iniquity, but thou hast delivered thy soul."[15]

This precept, I say, with the threatening annexed, together with the rest that is spoken in the same chapter, not to Ezekiel only, but to everyone whom God placeth watchman over his people and flock (and watchmen are they whose eyes he doth open and whose conscience he pricketh to admonish the ungodly), compelleth me to utter my conscience in this matter, notwithstanding that the whole world should be offended with me for so doing.

If any wonder why I do conceal my name, let him be assured that the fear of corporal punishment is neither the only, neither the chief cause. My purpose is thrice to blow the trumpet in the same matter, if God so permit. Twice I intend to do it without name, but at the last blast to take the blame upon myself, that all others may be purged.[16]

The First Blast To Awake Women Degenerate.

To promote a woman to bear rule, superiority, dominion, or empire above any realm, nation, or city is repugnant to nature, contumely to God, a thing most contrarious to his revealed will and approved ordinance, and, finally, it is the subversion of good order, of all equity and justice.

In the probation of this proposition I will not be so curious as to gather whatsoever may amplify, set forth, or decor the same; but I am purposed, even as I have spoken my conscience in most plain and few words, so to stand content with a simple proof of every member, bringing in for my witness God's ordinance in nature, his plain will revealed in his word, and the minds of such as be most ancient amongst godly writers.

And first, where that I affirm the empire of a woman to be a thing repugnant to nature, I mean not only that God by the order of his creation hath spoiled woman of authority and dominion, but also that man hath seen, proved, and pronounced just causes why that it so should be. Man, I say, in many other cases blind, doth in this behalf see very clearly, for the causes be so manifest that they cannot be hid. For who can deny but it repugneth to nature that the blind shall be appointed to lead and conduct such as do see, that the weak, the sick and impotent persons, shall nourish and keep the whole and strong, and, finally, that the foolish, mad, and frenetic shall govern the discrete and give counsel to such as be sober of mind? And such be all women compared unto man in bearing of authority. For their sight in civil regiment is but blindness, their counsel foolishness, and judgment frenzy, if it be rightly considered. I except such as God, by singular privilege and for certain causes known only to himself, hath exempted from the common rank of women, and do speak of women as nature and experience do this day declare them.

Nature, I say, doth paint them forth to be weak, frail, impatient, feeble, and foolish, and experience hath declared them to be unconstant, variable, cruel, and lacking the spirit of counsel and regiment. And these notable faults have men in all ages espied in that kind, for the which not only they have removed women from rule and authority, but also some have thought that men subject to the counsel or empire of their wives were unworthy of all public office. For thus writeth Aristotle in the second of his *Politics:* "What difference shall we put," saith he, "whether that women bear authority or the husbands that obey the empire of their wives be appointed to be magistrates? For what ensueth the one must needs follow the other, to wit, injustice, confusion, and disorder."[17] The same author further reasoneth that the policy or regiment of the Lacedemonians (who other ways amongst the Grecians were most excellent) was not worthy to be reputed nor accompted amongst the number of commonwealths that were well governed, because the magistrates and rulers of the same were too much given to please and obey their wives.

What would this writer, I pray you, have said to that realm or nation where a woman sitteth crowned in parliament amongst the midst of men? Oh fearful and terrible are thy judgments, O Lord, which thus hast abased man for his iniquity! I am assuredly persuaded that if any of those men, which illuminated only by the light of nature did see and pronounce causes sufficient why women ought not to bear rule nor authority, should this day live and see a woman sitting in judgment or riding from parliament in the midst of men, having the royal crown upon her head, the sword and scepter borne before her in sign that the administration of justice was in her power; I am assuredly persuaded, I say, that such a sight should so astonish them that they should judge the whole world to be transformed into Amazons, and that such a metamorphosis and change was made of all the men of that country (as poets do feign was made of the companions of Ulysses), or at least that albeit the outward form of men remained; yet should they judge that their hearts were changed from the wisdom, understanding, and courage of men to the foolish fondness and cowardice of women.[18] Yea, they further should pronounce that where women reign or be in authority that there must needs vanity be preferred to virtue, ambition and pride to temperance and modesty, and, finally, that avarice, the mother of all mischief, must needs devour equity and justice.[19]

But lest that we shall seem to be of this opinion alone, let us hear what others have seen and decreed in this matter. In the rules of the law thus it is written: "Women are removed from all civil and public office, so that they neither may be judged, neither may they occupy the place of the magistrate, neither yet may they be speakers for others."[20] The same is repeated in the third and in the sixteenth books of the *Digests* where certain persons are forbidden, *Ne pro aliis postulent,* that is, that they be no speakers nor advocates for others.[21] And among the rest are women forbidden, and this cause is added, that they do not against shamefastness intermeddle themselves with the causes of others, neither yet that women presume to use the offices due to men.[22] The law in the same place doth further declare that a natural shamefastness ought to be in womankind which most certainly she loseth whensoever she taketh upon her the office and estate of man.[23] As in Calpurnia was evidently declared, who, having license to speak before the Senate, at length became so impudent and importune that by her babbling she troubled the whole assembly and so gave occasion that this law was established.

In the first book of the *Digests* it is pronounced that the condition of the woman in many cases is worse than of the man.[24] As in jurisdiction, saith the law, in receiving of cure and tuition, in adoption, in public accusation, in declaration, in all popular action, and in motherly power, which she hath not upon her own sons.[25] The law further will not permit that the woman give anything to her husband, because it is against the nature of her kind, being the inferior member, to presume to give anything to her head. The law doth moreover pronounce womankind to be most avaricious, which is a vice intolerable in those that should rule or minister justice.[26] And Aristotle, as before is touched, doth plainly affirm that wheresoever women bear dominion there must needs the people be disordered, living and abounding in all intemperance, given to pride, excess, and vanity. And finally, in the end that they must needs come to confusion and ruin.[27]

Would to God the examples were not so manifest. To the further declaration of the imperfections of women, of their natural weak-

ness and inordinate appetites, I might adduce histories proving
some women to have died for sudden joy, some for unpatience to
have murdered themselves; some to have burned with such inordinate lust that, for the quenching of the same, they have betrayed to
strangers their country and city; and some to have been so desirous
of dominion that, for the obtaining of the same, they have murdered the children of their own sons. Yea, and some have killed
with cruelty their own husbands and children.[28] But to me it is
sufficient (because this part of nature is not my most sure foundation) to have proved that men, illuminated only by the light of
nature, have seen and have determined that it is a thing most
repugnant to nature that women rule and govern over men. For
those that will not permit a woman to have power over her own
sons will not permit her, I am assured, to have rule over a realm;
and those that will not suffer her to speak in defense of those that
be accused, neither that will admit her accusation intended against
man, will not approve her that she shall sit in judgment, crowned
with the royal crown, usurping authority in the midst of men.

But now to the second part of nature, in the which I include the
revealed will and perfect ordinance of God; and against this part of
nature, I say that it doth manifestly repugn that any woman shall
reign or bear dominion over man. For God, first by the order of
his creation and after by the curse and malediction pronounced
against the woman by the reason of her rebellion, hath pronounced
the contrary.

First, I say that woman in her greatest perfection was made to
serve and obey man, not to rule and command him. As St. Paul
doth reason in these words: "Man is not of the woman but the
woman of the man. And man was not created for the cause of the
woman, but the woman for the cause of man, and therefore ought
the woman to have a power upon her head"[29] (that is, a coverture in
sign of subjection). Of which words it is plain that the Apostle
meaneth that woman in her greatest perfection should have known
that man was lord above her, and therefore, that she should never
have pretended any kind of superiority above him no more than do
the angels above God the creator or above Christ Jesus their head.
So, I say that in her greatest perfection woman was created to be
subject to man.

But after her fall and rebellion committed against God there was
put upon her a new necessity, and she was made subject to man by
the irrevocable sentence of God pronounced in these words: "I will
greatly multiply thy sorrow and thy conception. With sorrow

shalt thou bear thy children, and thy will shall be subject to thy man, and he shall bear dominion over thee."[30] Hereby may such as altogether be not blinded plainly see that God by his sentence hath dejected all woman from empire and dominion above man. For two punishments are laid upon her, to wit, a dolor, anguish, and pain as oft as ever she shall be mother, and a subjection of herself, her appetites and will, to her husband and to his will. From the former part of the malediction can neither art, nobility, policy, nor law made by man deliver womankind; but whosoever attaineth to that honor to be mother proveth in experience the effect and strength of God's word.

But, alas, ignorance of God, ambition, and tyranny have studied to abolish and destroy the second part of God's punishment, for women are lifted up to be heads over realms and to rule above men at their pleasure and appetites. But horrible is the vengeance which is prepared for the one and for the other: for the promoters and for the persons promoted, except they speedily repent. For they shall be dejected from the glory of the sons of God to the slavery of the devil and to the torment that is prepared for all such as do exalt themselves against God. Against God nothing be more manifest than that a woman shall be exalted to reign above man. For the contrary sentence hath he pronounced in these words: "Thy will shall be subject to thy husband, and he shall bear dominion over thee."[31] As God should say: "Forasmuch as thou hast abused thy former condition, and because thy free will hath brought thyself and mankind into the bondage of Satan, I therefore will bring thee in bondage to man. For where before thy obedience should have been voluntary, now it shall be by constraint and by necessity; and that because thou hast deceived thy man, thou shalt therefore be no longer mistress over thine own appetites, over thine own will nor desires. For in thee there is neither reason nor discretion which be able to moderate thy affections, and therefore they shall be subject to the desire of thy man. He shall be lord and governor, not only over thy body, but even over thy appetites and will." This sentence, I say, did God pronounce against Eve and her daughters, as the rest of the Scriptures doth evidently witness. So that no woman can ever presume to reign over man, but the same she must needs do in despite of God and in contempt of his punishment and malediction.

I am not ignorant that the most part of men do understand this malediction of the subjection of the wife to her husband and of the dominion which he beareth above her; but the Holy Ghost giveth to us another interpretation of this place taking from all women all kind of superiority, authority, and power over man, speaking as followeth by the mouth of St. Paul: "I suffer not a woman to teach, neither yet to usurp authority above man."[32] Here he nameth women in general, excepting none, affirming that she may usurp authority above no man. And that he speaketh more plainly in another place in these words: "Let women keep silence in the congregation, for it is not permitted to them to speak, but to be subject as the law saith."[33] These two testimonies of the Holy Ghost be sufficient to prove whatsoever we have affirmed before and to repress the inordinate pride of women, as also to correct the foolishness of those that have studied to exalt women in authority above man, against God, and against his sentence pronounced.

But that the same two places of the Apostle may the better be understand, it is to be noted that in the latter, which is written in the First Epistle to the Corinthians, the fourteenth chapter, before the Apostle had permitted that all persons should prophesy one after another, adding this reason: "that all may learn and all may receive consolation." And lest that any might have judged that amongst a rude multitude and the plurality of speakers many things, little to purpose, might have been affirmed, or else that some confusion might have risen, he addeth: "the spirits of the prophets are subject to the prophets." As he should say, God shall always raise up some to whom the verity shall be revealed, and unto such ye shall give place, albeit they sit in the lowest seats. And thus the Apostle would have prophesying an exercise to be free to the whole church, that everyone should communicate with the congregation what God have revealed to them, providing that it were orderly done.

But from this general privilege he secludeth all woman, saying, "Let women keep silence in the congregation." And why, I pray you, was it because that the Apostle thought no woman to have any knowledge? No, he giveth another reason, saying, "Let her be subject as the law saith." In which words is first to be noted that the Apostle calleth this former sentence pronounced against woman a law, that is, the immutable decree of God, who by his own voice hath subjected her to one member of the congregation, that is, to her husband. Whereupon the Holy Ghost concludeth that she may never rule nor bear empire above man. For she that is made subject to one may never be preferred to many, and that the Holy Ghost doth manifestly express, saying, "I suffer not that woman usurp authority above man." He saith not, "I will not that woman usurp authority above her husband," but he nameth man in general, taking from her all power and authority to speak, to reason, to interpret, or to teach, but principally, to rule or to judge in the assembly of men. So that woman, by the law of God and by the interpretation of the Holy Ghost, is utterly forbidden to occupy the place of God in the offices aforesaid, which he hath assigned to man, whom he hath appointed and ordained his lieutenant in earth, secluding from that honor and dignity all woman, as this short argument shall evidently declare.

The Apostle taketh power from all woman to speak in the assembly. *Ergo,* he permitteth no woman to rule above man. The former part is evident, whereupon doth the conclusion of necessity follow. For he that taketh from woman the least part of authority, dominion, or rule will not permit unto her that which is greatest. But greater it is to reign above realms and nations, to publish and to make laws, and to command men of all estates, and, finally, to appoint judges and ministers, than to speak in the congregation. For her judgment, sentence, or opinion, proposed in the congregation, may be judged by all, may be corrected by the learned and reformed by the godly. But woman, being promoted in sovereign authority, her laws must be obeyed, her opinion followed, and her tyranny maintained, supposing that it be expressly against God and the profit of the commonwealth, as to manifest experience doth this day witness. And therefore, yet again, I repeat that which before I have affirmed, to wit, that a woman promoted to sit in the seat of God, that is, to teach, to judge, or to reign above man, is a monster in nature, contumely to God, and a thing most repugnant to his will and ordinance. For he hath deprived them, as before is proved, of speaking in the congregation and hath expressly forbidden them to usurp any kind of authority above man.

How then will he suffer them to reign and have empire above realms and nations? He will neither, I say, approve it, because it is a thing most repugnant to his perfect ordinance, as after shall be declared and as the former Scriptures have plainly given testimony. To the which to add anything were superfluous were it not that the world is almost now comen to that blindness that whatsoever pleaseth not the princes and the multitude, the same is rejected as doctrine newly forged and is condemned for heresy. I have therefore thought good to recite the minds of some ancient writers in the same matter, to the end that such as altogether be not blinded by the devil may consider and understand this my judgment to be no new interpretation of God's Scripture but to be the uniform consent of the most part of godly writers since the time of the Apostles.

Tertullian, in his book of women's apparel, after that he hath shewed many causes why gorgeous apparel is abominable and odious in a woman, addeth these words, speaking, as it were, to every woman by name: "Dost thou not know," saith he, "that thou art Eve? The sentence of God liveth and is effectual against this kind, and in this world of necessity it is that the punishment also live. Thou art the port and gate of the devil. Thou art the first transgressor of God's law; thou didst persuade and easily deceive him whom the devil durst not assault. For thy merit (that is for thy death) it behooved the son of God to suffer the death, and doth it yet abide in thy mind to deck thee above thy skin coats?"[34] By these and many other grave sentences and quick interrogations did this godly writer labor to bring every woman in contemplation of herself, to the end that every one, deeply weighing what sentence God had pronounced against the whole race and daughters of Eve, might not only learn daily to humble and subject themselves in the presence of God, but also that they should avoid and abhor whatsoever thing might exalt them or puff them up in pride, or that might be occasion that should forget the curse and malediction of God.

And what, I pray you, is more able to cause woman to forget her own condition than if she be lifted up in authority above man? It is a thing very difficile to a man (be he never so constant) promoted to honors not to be tickled somewhat with pride (for the wind of vainglory doth easily carry up the dry dust of the earth). But as for woman, it is no more possible that she, being set aloft in authority above man, shall resist the motions of pride than it is able to the weak reed or to the turning weathercock not to bow or turn at the vehemency of the unconstant wind. And therefore the same writer expressly forbiddeth all women to intermeddle with the office of man. For thus he writeth in his book *de virginibus velandis*: "It is not permitted to a woman to speak in the congregation, neither to teach, neither to baptize, neither to vindicate to herself any office of man."[35] The same he speaketh yet more plainly in the preface of his sixth book written against Marcion, where he recounting certain monstrous things which were to be seen at the sea called *Euxinum*. Amongst the rest he reciteth this as a great monster in nature, that "woman in those parts were not tamed nor embased by consideration of their own sex and kind; but that all shame laid apart, they made expenses upon weapons and learned the feats of war, having more pleasure to fight than to marry and be subject to man."[36] Thus far of Tertullian, whose words be so plain that they need no explanation. For he that taketh from her all office appertaining to man will not suffer her to reign above man; and he that judgeth it a monster in nature that a woman shall exercise weapons must judge it to be a monster that a woman shall be exalted above a whole realm and nation. Of the same mind is Origen and divers others. Yea, even till the days of Augustine, whose sentences I omit to avoid prolixity.

Augustine in his twenty-second book written against Faustus proveth that a woman ought serve her husband as unto God, affirming that in no thing hath woman equal power with man, saving that neither of both have power over their own bodies.[37] By which he would plainly conclude that woman ought never to pretend nor thirst for that power and authority which is due to man. For so he doth explain himself in another place: affirming that woman ought to be repressed and bridled betimes, if she aspire to any dominion; alleging that dangerous and perilous it is to suffer her to proceed, although it be in temporal and corporal things. And thereto he addeth these words: "God seeth not for a time, neither is there any new thing in his sight and knowledge"[38]— meaning thereby that what God hath seen in one woman, as concerning dominion and bearing of authority, the same he seeth in all. And what he hath forbidden to one, the same he also forbiddeth to all. And this most evidently yet in another place he writeth, moving this question: "How can woman be the image of God, seeing," saith he, "she is subject to man and hath none authority, neither to teach, neither to be witness, neither to judge, much less to rule or bear empire?"[39] These be the very words of Augustine, of which it is evident that this godly writer doth not only agree with Tertullian, before recited, but also with the former sentence of the law which taketh from woman not only all authority amongst men but also every office appertaining to man.

To the question how she can be the image of God, he answereth as followeth. "Woman," saith he, "compared to other creatures is the image of God, for she beareth dominion over them; but compared unto man, she may not be called the image of God, for she beareth not rule and lordship over man, but to obey him," etc. And how that woman ought to obey man, he speaketh yet more clearly in these words: "The woman shall be subject to man as unto Christ." "For woman", saith he, "hath not her example from the body and from the flesh, that so she shall be subject to man as the flesh is unto the spirit. Because that the flesh in the weakness and mortality of this life striveth and striveth against the spirit, and therefore would not the Holy Ghost give example of subjection to the woman of any such thing," etc.[40] This sentence of Augustine ought to be noted of all women, for in it he plainly affirmeth that woman ought to be subject to man, that she never ought more to desire pre-eminence above him than that she ought to desire above Christ Jesus.

With Augustine agreeth in every point St. Ambrose, who thus writeth in his *Hexameron*: "Adam was deceived by Eve, and not Eve by Adam, and therefore just it is that woman receive and acknowledge him for governor whom she called to sin, lest that again she slide and fall by womanly facility."[41] And writing upon the Epistle to the Ephesians, he saith, "Let women be subject to their own husbands as unto the Lord; for the man is head to the woman, and Christ is head to the congregation, and he is the savior of the body; but the congregation is subject to Christ; even so ought women to be to their husbands in all things." He proceedeth further, saying, "Women are commanded to be subject to men by the law of nature, because that man is the author or beginner of the woman; for as Christ is head of the church, so is man of the woman. From Christ the church took beginning, and therefore it is subject unto him; even so did woman take beginning from man that she should be subject."[42]

Thus we hear the agreeing of these two writers to be such that a man might judge the one to have stolen the words and sentences from the other, and yet, plain it is that, during the time of their writing, the one was far distant from the other. But the Holy Ghost, who is the spirit of concord and unity, did so illuminate their hearts and direct their tongues and pens that, as they did conceive and understand one truth, so they did pronounce and utter the same, leaving a testimony of their knowledge and posterity.

If any think that all these former sentences be spoken only of the subjection of the married woman to her husband, as before I have proved the contrary by the plain words and reasoning of St. Paul, so shall I shortly do the same by other testimony of the foresaid writers. The same Ambrose, writing upon the second chapter of the First Epistle to Timothy, after he hath spoken much of the simple arrayment of women, he addeth these words: "Woman ought not only to have simple arrayment, but all authority is to be denied unto her, for she must be in subjection to man, of whom she hath taken her original, as well in habit as in service." And after a few words he saith, "Because that death did enter into the world by her, there is no boldness that ought to be permitted unto her, but she ought to be in humility."[43] Hereof it is plain that from all woman, be she married or unmarried, is all authority taken to execute any office that appertaineth to man. Yea, plain it is that all woman is commanded to serve, to be in humility and subjection. Which thing yet speaketh the same writer more plainly in these words: "It is not permitted to women to speak, but to be in silence, as the law saith. What saith the law? 'Unto thy husband shall thy conversion be, and he shall bear dominion over thee.' This is a special law," saith Ambrose, "whose sentence, lest it should be violated, infirmed, or made weak, women are commanded to be in silence." Here he includeth all women. And yet he proceedeth further in the same place, saying, "It is shame for them to presume to speak of the law in the house of the Lord who hath commanded them to be subject to their men."[44, 45]

But most plainly speaketh he writing upon the sixteenth chapter of the Epistle of St. Paul to the Romans, upon these words: "Salute Rufus and his mother." "For this cause," saith Ambrose, "did the Apostle place Rufus before his mother, for the election of the administration of the grace of God, in which a woman hath no place. For he was chosen and promoted by the Lord to take care over his business, that is, over the church, to which office could not his mother be appointed, albeit she was a woman so holy that the Apostle called her his mother." Hereof it is plain that the administration of the grace of God is denied to all woman. By the administration of God's grace is understand not only the preaching of the word and administration of the sacraments, by the which the grace of God is presented and ordinarily distributed unto man, but also the administration of civil justice, by the which virtue ought to be maintained and vices punished. The execution whereof is no less denied to woman than is the preaching of the Evangel or administration of the sacraments, as hereafter shall most plainly appear.

Chrysostom, amongst the Grecian writers of no small credit, speaking in rebuke of men who in his days were becomen inferior to some women in wit and in godliness, saith, "For this cause was woman put under thy power" (he speaketh to man in general), "and thou wast pronounced lord over her that she should obey thee and that the head should not follow the feet. But often it is that we see the contrary; that he who is his order ought to be the head, doth not keep the order of the feet (that is, doth not rule the feet) and she, that is in place of the foot, is constitute to be the head."[46] He speaketh these words as it were in admiration that man was becomen so brutish that he did not consider it to be a thing most monstrous that woman should be preferred to man in anything, whom God had subjected to man in all things. He proceedeth, saying, "Nevertheless, it is the part of the man with diligent care to repel the woman that giveth him wicked counsel; and woman which gave that pestilent counsel to man ought at all times to have the punishment which was given to Eve sounding in her ears." And in another place he induceth God, speaking to the woman in this sort: "Because thou left him, of whose nature thou was participant and for whom thou wast formed, and hast had pleasure to have familiarity with that wicked beast and would take his counsel; therefore, I subject thee to man, and I appoint and affirm him to be thy lord that thou mayest acknowledge his dominion; and because thou couldst not bear rule, learn well to be ruled."[47] Why they should not bear rule, he declareth in other places, saying, "Womankind is imprudent and soft or flexible. Imprudent because she cannot consider with wisdom and reason the things which she heareth and seeth; and soft she is because she is easily bowed."[48]

Chrysostom bringeth in these words to declare the cause why false prophets do commonly deceive women: because they are easily persuaded to any opinion, especially if it be against God, and because they lack prudence and right reason to judge the things that be spoken. But hereof may their nature be espied, and the vices of the same, which in nowise ought to be in those that are appointed to govern others. For they ought to be constant, stable, prudent, and doing everything with discretion and reason, which virtues women cannot have in equality with men. For that he doth witness in another place, saying, "Women have in themselves a tickling and study of vainglory, and that they may have common with men; they are suddenly moved to anger, and that they may have also common with some men. But virtues in which they excel they have not common with man, and therefore hath the Apostle removed them from the office of teaching, which is an evident proof that in virtue they far differ from man." Let the reasons of this writer be marked, for further he yet proceedeth, after that he hath in many words lamented the effeminate manners of men who were so far degenerate to the weakness of women that some might have demanded: why may not women teach amongst such a sort of men who in wisdom and godliness are become inferior unto woman? He finally concludeth, "That notwithstanding that men be degenerate, yet may not women usurp any authority above them." And in the end he addeth these words: "These things do not I speak to extol them (that is, women) but to the confusion and shame of ourselves, and to admonish us to take again the dominion that is meet and convenient for us, not only that power which is according to providence and according to help and virtue. For then is the body in best proportion when it hath the best governor."[49]

O, that both man and woman should consider the profound counsel and admonition of this father! He would not that man for appetite of any vainglory should desire pre-eminence above woman, for God hath not made man to be head for any such cause. But having respect to that weakness and imperfection which always letteth woman to govern, he hath ordained man to be superior; and that meaneth Chrysostom, saying, "Then is the body in best proportion when it hath the best governor. But woman can never be the best governor by reason that she, being spoiled of the spirit of regiment, can never attain to that degree to be called or judged a good governor; because in the nature of all woman lurketh such vices as in good governors are not tolerable."[50] Which the same writer expresseth in these words: "Womankind," saith he, "is rash and foolhardy, and their covetousness is like the gulf of hell, that is, insatiable."[51] And therefore in another place, he will that woman shall have nothing to do in judgment, in common affairs, or in the regiment of the commonwealth, because she is impatient of troubles, but that she shall live in tranquillity and quietness. And if she have occasion to go from the house, that yet she shall have no matter of trouble, neither to follow her, neither to be offered unto her, as commonly there must be to such as bear authority.

And with Chrysostom fully agreeth Basilius Magnus in a sermon which he maketh upon some places of Scripture, wherein he reproveth divers vices, and amongst the rest he affirmeth woman to be a tender creature, flexible, soft, and pitiful, which nature God hath given unto her that she may be apt to nourish children. The which facility of the woman did Satan abuse and thereby brought her from the obedience of God. And therefore in divers other places doth he conclude that she is not apt to bear rule and that she is forbidden to teach.[52]

Innumerable more testimonies of all sorts of writers may be adduced for the same purpose, but with these I stand content: judging it sufficient to stop the mouth of such as accuse and condemn all doctrine as heretical which displeaseth them in any point, that I have proved by the determinations and laws of men illuminated only by the light of nature, by the order of God's creation, by the curse and malediction pronounced against woman by the mouth of St. Paul, who is the interpreter of God's sentence and law, and finally, by the minds of those writers who in the church of God have been always holden in greatest reverence, that it is a thing most repugnant to nature, to God's will and appointed ordinance (yea, that it cannot be without contumely committed against God), that a woman should be promoted to dominion or empire to reign over man, be it in realm, nation, province, or city. Now resteth it in few words to be shewed that the same empire of women is the subversion of good order, equity, and justice.

Augustine defineth order to be that thing by which God hath appointed and ordained all things.[53] Note well, reader, that Augustine will admit no order where God's appointment is absent and lacketh. And in another place he saith, that "order is a disposition, giving their own proper places in things that be unequal," which he termeth in Latin *parium et disparium,* that is, of things equal or like and things unequal or unlike.[54] Of which two places and of the whole disputation, which is contained in his second book *De ordine,* it is evident that whatsoever is done either without the assurance of God's will, or else against his will manifestly revealed in his word, is done against order. But such is the empire and regiment of all woman (as evidently before is declared); and therefore I say, it is a thing plainly repugnant to good order, yea, it is the subversion of the same.

If any list to reject the definition of Augustine, as either not proper to this purpose or else as insufficient to prove mine intent, let the same man understand that in so doing he hath infirmed mine argument nothing. For as I depend not upon the determinations of men, so think I my cause no weaker, albeit their authority be denied unto me, provided that God, by his will revealed and manifest word, stand plain and evident on my side. That God hath subjected womankind to man by the order of his creation and by the curse that he hath pronounced against her is before declared.

Besides these, he hath set before our eyes two other mirrors and glasses, in which he will that we should behold the order which he hath appointed and established in nature. The one is the natural body of man; the other is the politic or civil body of that commonwealth in which God by his own word hath appointed an order.

In the natural body of man God hath appointed an order that the head shall occupy the uppermost place. And the head hath he joined with the body, that from it doth life and motion flow to the rest of the members. In it hath he placed the eye to see, the ear to hear, and the tongue to speak—which offices are appointed to none other member of the body. The rest of the members have every one their own place and office appointed, but none may have neither the place nor office of the head. For who would not judge that body to be a monster where there was no head eminent above the rest, but that the eyes were in the hands, the tongue and mouth beneath in the belly, and the ears in the feet? Men, I say, should not only pronounce this body to be a monster, but, assuredly, they might conclude that such a body could not long endure.

And no less monstrous is the body of that commonwealth where a woman beareth empire; for either doth it lack a lawful head (as in very deed it doth), or else there is an idol exalted in the place of the true head. An idol I call that which hath the form and appearance but lacketh the virtue and strength which the name and proportion do resemble and promise. As images have face, nose, eyes, mouth, hands, and feet painted, but the use of the same cannot the craft and art of man give them. As the Holy Ghost by the mouth of David teacheth us, saying, "They have eyes, but they see not, mouth, but they speak not, nose, but they smell not, hands and feet, but they neither touch nor have power to go."[55] And such, I say, is every realm and nation where a woman beareth dominion. For in despite of God (he of his just judgment so giving them over into a reprobate mind), may a realm, I confess, exalt up a woman to that monstriferous honor to be esteemed as head. But impossible it is to man and angel to give unto her the properties and perfect offices of a lawful head. For the same God that hath denied power to the hand to speak, to the belly to hear, and to the feet to see, hath denied to woman power to command man and hath taken away wisdom to consider and to foresee the things that be profitable to the commonwealth. Yea, finally, he hath denied to her in any case to be head to man, but plainly hath pronounced that "man is head to woman, even as Christ is head to all man."[56] If men in a blind rage should assemble together and appoint themselves another head than Jesus Christ (as the papists have done their romish Antichrist), should Christ, therefore, lose his own dignity, or should God give to that counterfeit head power to give life to the body, to see whatsoever might endamage or hurt it, to speak in defense, and to hear the request of every subject? It is certain that he would not. For that honor he hath appointed before all times to his only son, and the same he will give to no creature besides. No more will he admit nor accept woman to be the lawful head over man, although man, devil, and angel will conjure in their favor. For seeing he hath subjected her to one, as before is said, he will never permit her to reign over many. Seeing he hath commanded her to hear and obey one, he will not suffer that she speak and with usurped authority command realms and nations.

Chrysostom, explaining these words of the Apostle, "the head of woman is man," compareth God in his universal regiment to a king sitting in his royal majesty to whom all his subjects, commanded to give homage and obedience, appear before him, bearing every one such a badge and cognizance of dignity and honor as he hath given to them (which if they despise and condemn, then do they dishonor their king). "Even so," saith he, "ought man and woman to appear before God, bearing the ensigns of the condition which they have received of him. Man hath received a certain glory and dignity above the woman, and therefore ought he to appear before his high majesty, bearing the sign of his honor, having no coverture upon his head to witness that in earth men hath no head." Beware Chrysostom what thou sayest; thou shalt be reputed a traitor if Englishmen hear thee, for they must have my sovereign lady and mistress, and Scotland hath drunken also the enchantment and venom of Circes. Let it be so to their own shame. He proceedeth in these words: "but woman ought to be covered to witness that in earth she hath a head, that is, man." True it is, Chrysostom, woman is covered in both the said realms, but it is not with the sign of subjection, but it is with the sign of superiority, to wit, with the royal crown. To that he answereth in these words: "What if man neglect his honor? He is no less to be mocked," saith Chrysostom, "than if a king should depose himself of his diadem or crown and royal estate, and clothe himself in the habit of a slave."[57]

What, I pray you, should this godly father have said if he had seen all the men of a realm or nation fall down before a woman? If he had seen the crown, scepter, and sword, which are ensigns of the royal dignity, given to her; and a woman, cursed of God and made subject to man, placed in the throne of justice to sit as God's lieutenant? What, I say in his behalf, should any heart, unfeignedly fearing God, have judged of such men? I am assured that not only should they have been judged foolish, but also enraged and slaves to Satan, manifestly fighting against God and his appointed order.

The more that I consider the subversion of God's order, which he hath placed generally in all living things, the more I do wonder at the blindness of man, who doth not consider himself in this case so degenerate that the brute beasts are to be preferred unto him in this behalf. For nature hath in all beasts printed a certain mark of dominion in the male and a certain subjection in the female which they keep inviolate. For no man ever saw the lion to make obedience and stoop before the lioness, neither yet can it be proved that the hind taketh the conducting of the herd amongst the harts. And yet, alas, man, who by the mouth of God hath dominion appointed to him over woman, doth not only to his own shame stoop under the obedience of women, but also, in despite of God and his appointed order, rejoiceth and maintaineth that monstrous authority as a thing lawful and just.

The insolent joy, the bonfires, and banqueting which were in London and elsewhere in England when that cursed Jezebel was proclaimed Queen did witness to my heart that men were becomen more than enraged. For else how could they so have rejoiced at their own confusion and certain destruction? For what man was there of so base judgment, supposing that he had any light of God, who did not see the erecting of that monster to be the overthrow of true religion and the assured destruction of England and of the ancient liberties thereof? And yet, nevertheless, all men so triumphed as if God had delivered them from all calamity.

But just and righteous, terrible and fearful are thy judgments, O Lord![58] For as sometimes thou didst so punish men for unthankfulness, that man ashamed not to commit villainy with man, and that because that knowing thee to be God, they glorified thee not as God, even so hast thou most justly now punished the proud rebellion and horrible ingratitude of the realms of England and Scotland. For when thou didst offer thyself most mercifully to them both, offering the means by the which they might have been joined together forever in godly concord, then was the one proud and cruel and the other unconstant and fickle of promise. But yet, alas, did miserable England further rebel against thee. For albeit thou didst not cease to heap benefit upon benefit during the reign of an innocent and tender king, yet no man did acknowledge thy potent hand and marvelous working.

The stout courage of captains, the wit and policy of councillors, the learning of bishops, did rob thee of thy glory and honor. For what then was heard as concerning religion, but the king's proceedings, the king's proceedings must be obeyed? It is enacted by parliament; therefore it is treason to speak in the contrary. But this was not the end of this miserable tragedy. For thou didst yet proceed to offer thy favors, sending thy prophets and messengers to call for reformation of life in all estates. For even from the highest to the lowest all were declined from thee (yea, even those that should have been the lanterns to others); some, I am assured, did quake and tremble, and from the bottom of their hearts thirsted amendment, and for the same purpose did earnestly call for discipline. But then burst forth the venom which before lurked; then might they not contain their despiteful voices, but with open mouths did cry: we will not have such a one to reign over us.

Then, I say, was every man so stout that he would not be brought in bondage, no, not to thee, O Lord; but with disdain did the multitude cast from them the amiable yoke of Christ Jesus. No man would suffer his sin to be rebuked, no man would have his life called to trial. And thus did they refuse thee, O Lord, and thy son Christ Jesus to be their pastor, protector, and prince. And therefore hast thou given them over into a reprobate mind. Thou hast taken from them the spirit of boldness, of wisdom, and of righteous judgment. They see their own destruction, and yet they have no grace to avoid it. Yea, they are becomen so blind that, knowing the pit, they headlong cast themselves into the same, as the nobility of England do this day, fighting in the defense of their mortal enemy, the Spaniard. Finally, they are so destitute of understanding and judgment that, although they know that there is a liberty and freedom the which their predecessors have enjoyed, yet are they compelled to bow their necks under the yoke of Satan, and of his proud ministers, pestilent papists, and proud Spaniards. And yet can they not consider that where a woman reigneth and papists bear authority, that there must needs Satan be president of the council? Thus hast thou, O Lord, in thy hot displeasure revenged the contempt of thy graces offered.[59]

But, O Lord, if thou shalt retain wrath to the end, what flesh is able to sustain? We have sinned, O Lord, and are not worthy to be relieved. But worthy art thou, O Lord, to be a true God, and worthy is thy son Christ Jesus to have his Evangel and glory advanced; which both are trodden underfoot in this cruel murder and persecution, which the builders of Babylon commit in their fury have raised against thy children for the establishing of their kingdom. Let the sobs, therefore, of thy prisoners, O Lord, pass up to thine ears; consider their affliction, and let the eyes of thy mercy look down upon the blood of such as die for testimony of thy eternal verity, and let not thine enemies mock thy judgment forever. To thee, O Lord, I turn my wretched and wicked heart, to thee alone I direct my complaint and groans; for in that isle to thy saints there is left no comfort.

Albeit I have thus, talking with my God in the anguish of my heart, somewhat digressed, yet have I not utterly forgotten my former proposition, to wit, that it is a thing repugnant to the order of nature that any woman be exalted to rule over men, for God hath denied unto her the office of a head. And in the entreating of this part, I remember that I have made the nobility both of England and Scotland inferior to brute beasts, for that they do to women which no male amongst the common sort of beasts can be proved to do to their females, that is, they reverence them, and quake at their presence, they obey their commandments, and that against God. Wherefore I judge them not only subjects to women, but slaves to Satan and servants of iniquity. If any man think these my words sharp or vehement, let him consider that the offense is more heinous than can be expressed by words. For where all things be expressedly concluded against the glory and honor of God, and where the blood of the saints of God is commanded to be shed, whom shall we judge, God or the devil, to be president of that council? Plain it is, that God ruleth not by his love, mercy, nor grace in the assembly of the ungodly. Then it resteth that the devil, the prince of this world, doth reign over such tyrants. Whose servants, I pray you, shall then be judged such as obey and execute their tyranny? God, for his great mercy's sake, illuminate the eyes of men that they may perceive into what miserable bondage they be brought by the monstriferous empire of women.

The second glass which God hath set before the eyes of man wherein he may behold the order which pleaseth his wisdom concerning authority and dominion is that commonwealth to the which it pleaseth his majesty to appoint and give laws, statutes, rites, and ceremonies, not only concerning religion, but also touching their policy[60] and regiment of the same. And against that order it doth manifestly repugn that any woman shall occupy the throne of God, that is, the royal seat, which he by his word hath appointed to man. As in giving the law to Israel, concerning the election of a king, is evident, for thus it is written: "If thou shalt say, I will appoint a king above me, as the rest of the nations which are about me, thou shalt make thee a king whom the Lord thy God shall choose: one from amongst the midst of thy brethren, thou shalt appoint king above thee. Thou mayest not make a stranger that is not thy brother."[61] Here expressedly is a man appointed to be chosen king, and a man native amongst themselves, by which precept is all woman and all stranger secluded. What may be objected for the part or election of a stranger, shall be, God willing, answered in *The Blast of the Second Trumpet.* For this present, I say that the erecting of a woman to that honor is not only to invert the order which God hath established, but also is to defile, pollute, and profane (so far as in man lieth) the throne and seat of God, which he hath sanctified and appointed for man only, in the course of this wretched life, to occupy and possess as his minister and lieutenant, secluding from the same all woman, as before is expressed.

If any think that the forewritten law did bind the Jews only, let the same man consider that the election of a king and appointing of judges did neither appertain to the ceremonial law, neither yet was it mere judicial, but that it did flow from the moral law as an ordinance having respect to the conservation of both the tables. For the office of the magistrate ought to have the first and chief respect to the glory of God, commanded and contained in the former table, as is evident by that which was enjoined to Joshua by God, what time he was accepted and admitted ruler and governor over his people, in these words: "Thou shalt divide the inheritance to this people, the which I have sworn to their fathers, to give unto them: so that thou be valiant and strong, that thou mayest keep and do according to that whole law which my servant Moses hath commanded thee; thou shalt not decline from it, neither to the right hand, neither to the left hand, that thou mayest do prudently in all things that thou takest in hand. Let not the book of this law depart from thy mouth, but meditate in it day and night, that thou mayest keep and do according to everything that is written in it. For then shall thy ways prosper, and then shall thou do prudently," etc.[62] And the same precept giveth God by the mouth of Moses to kings, after they be elected, in these words: "When he shall sit in the throne or seat of his kingdom, he shall write to himself a copy of this law in a book, and that shall be with him that he may read in it all the days of his life, that he may learn to fear the Lord his God, and to keep all the words of this law and all these statutes, that he may do them," etc.[63] Of these two places it is evident that principally it appertaineth to the king or the chief magistrate to know the will of God, to be instructed in his law and statutes, and to promote his glory with his whole heart and study—which be the chief points of the first table.

No man denieth but that the word is committed to the magistrate to the end that he should punish vice and maintain virtue. To punish vice, I say, not only that which troubleth the tranquillity and quiet estate of the commonwealth by adultery, theft, or murder committed, but also such vices as openly impugn the glory of God, as idolatry, blasphemy, and manifest heresy, taught and obstinately maintained. As the histories and notable acts of Hezekiah, Jehoshaphat, and Josiah do plainly teach us, whose study and care was not only to glorify God in their own life and conversation, but also they unfeignedly did travail to bring their subjects to the true worshipping and honoring of God, and did destroy all monuments of idolatry, did punish to death the teachers of it, and removed from office and honors such as were maintainers of those abominations. Whereby I suppose that it be evident that the office of the king or supreme magistrate hath respect to the law moral and to the conservation of both the tables.

Now if the law moral be the constant and unchangeable will of God, to the which the gentile is no less bound than was the Jew; and if God will that amongst the gentiles, the ministers and executors of his law be now appointed as sometimes they were appointed amongst the Jews; further, if the execution of justice be no less requisite in the policy of the gentiles than ever it was amongst the Jews, what man can be so foolish to suppose or believe that God will now admit those persons to sit in judgment or to reign over men in the commonwealth of the gentiles whom he by his expressed word and ordinance did before debar and seclude from the same? And that women were secluded from the royal seat—the which ought to be the sanctuary to all poor afflicted, and therefore is justly called the seat of God (besides the place before recited of the election of a king, and besides the places of the New Testament which be most evident)—the order and election which was kept in Judah and Israel doth manifestly declare. For when the males of the kingly stock failed, as oft as it chanced in Israel and sometimes in Judah, it never entered into the hearts of the people to choose and promote to honors any of the king's daughters (had he never so many); but, knowing God's vengeance to be poured forth upon the father by the away taking of his sons, they had no further respect to his stock but elected such one man or other as they judged most apt for that honor and authority. Of which premises I conclude, as before, that to promote a woman head over men is repugnant to nature and a thing most contrarious to that order which God hath approved in that commonwealth which he did institute and rule by his word.

But now to the last point, to wit, that the empire of a woman is a thing repugnant to justice and the destruction of every common-wealth where it is received. In probation whereof, because the matter is more than evident, I will use few words. First, I say, if justice be a constant and perpetual will to give to every person their own right, as the most learned in all ages have defined it to be, then to give or to will to give to any person that which is not their right must repugn to justice. But to reign above man can never be the right to woman, because it is a thing denied unto her by God, as is before declared. Therefore, to promote her to that estate or dig-nity, can be nothing else but repugnancy to justice. If I should speak no more, this were sufficient; for except that either they can improve the definition of justice, or else that they can entreat God to revoke and call back his sentence pronounced against woman, they shall be compelled to admit my conclusion. If any find fault with justice as it is defined, he may well accuse others, but me he shall not hurt. For I have the shield, the weapon, and the warrant of him, who assuredly will defend his quarrel, and he commandeth me to cry: "Whatsoever repugneth the will of God expressed in his most sacred word, repugneth to justice; but that woman have authority over men, repugneth to the will of God expressed in his word; and therefore mine author commandeth me to conclude without fear that all such authority repugneth to justice."

The first part of the argument, I trust, dare neither Jew nor gentile deny. For it is a principle not only universally confessed, but also so deeply printed in the heart of man, be his nature never so corrupted, that, whether he will or no he is compelled at one time or other to acknowledge and confess that justice is violated when things are done against the will of God expressed by his word. And to this confession are no less the reprobate coacted and constrained than be the chosen children of God, albeit to a divers end. The elect, with displeasure of their fact, confess their offense, having access to grace and mercy, as did Adam, David, Peter, and all other penitent offenders. But the reprobate, notwithstanding they are compelled to acknowledge the will of God to be just the which they have offended; yet are they never inwardly displeased with their iniquity, but rage, complain, and storm against God, whose vengeance they cannot escape—as did Cain, Judas, Herod, Julian called Apostate, yea, Jezebel and Athaliah. For Cain no doubt was convict in conscience that he had done against justice in murdering of his brother.[64] Judas did openly before the high priest confess that he had sinned in betraying innocent blood.[65] Herod, being stricken by the angel, did mock those his flatterers, saying unto them, "Behold your God" (meaning of himself) "cannot now preserve himself from corruption and worms."[66] Julianus was compelled in the end to cry, "O Galilean" (so always in contempt did he name our savior Jesus Christ), "thou hast now overcomen." And who doubteth but Jezebel and Athaliah, before their miserable end, were convicted in their cankered consciences to acknowledge that the murder which they had committed and empire which the one had six years usurped were repugnant to justice.

Even so shall they, I doubt not, which this day do possess and maintain that monstriferous authority of women shortly be compelled to acknowledge that their studies and devises have been bent against God; and that all such authority as women have usurped repugneth to justice, because, as I have said, it repugneth to the will of God expressed in his sacred word. And if any man doubt hereof, let him mark well the words of the Apostle, saying, "I permit not a woman to teach, neither yet to usurp authority above man."[67] No man, I trust, will deny these words of the Apostle to be the will of God expressed in his word. And he saith openly, "I permit not," etc., which is as much as "I will not," that a woman have authority, charge, or power over man, for so much importeth the Greek word αὐθεντετν[68] in that place. Now let man and angel conspire against God, let them pronounce their laws, and say, "we will suffer women to bear authority, who then can depose them?" Yet shall this one word of the eternal God, spoken by the mouth of a weak man, thrust them every one into hell. Jezebel may for a time sleep quietly in the bed of her fornication and whoredom, she may teach and deceive for a season; but neither shall she preserve herself, neither yet her adulterous children, from great affliction and from the sword of God's vengeance which shall shortly apprehend such works of iniquity.[69] The admonition I defer to the end.

Here might I bring in the oppression and injustice which is committed against realms and nations, which sometimes lived free and now are brought in bondage of foreign nations, by the reason of this monstriferous authority and empire of women. But that I delay till better opportunity. And now I think it expedient to answer such objections as carnal and worldly men, yea, men ignorant of God, use to make for maintenance of this tyranny (authority it is not worthy to be called) and most unjust empire of woman. First, they do object the examples of Deborah and of Huldah the prophetess, of whom the one judged Israel and the other, by all appearance, did teach and exhort.[70] Secondarily, they do object the law made by Moses for the daughters of Zelophehad.[71] Thirdly, the consent of the estates of such realms as have approved the empire and regiment of women. And last, the long custom, which hath received the regiment of women, their valiant acts and prosperity, together with some papistical laws which have confirmed the same.

To the first, I answer that particular examples do establish no common law. The causes were known to God alone: why he took the spirit of wisdom and force from all men of those ages and did so mightily assist women, against nature and against his ordinary course, that the one he made a deliverer to his afflicted people of Israel, and to the other he gave not only perseverance in the true religion, when the most part of men had declined from the same, but also to her he gave the spirit of prophecy, to assure King Josiah of the things which were to come. With these two women, I say, did God work potently and miraculously; yea, to them he gave most singular grace and privilege. But who hath commanded that a public, yea, a tyrannical and most wicked law be established upon these examples?

The men that object the same are not altogether ignorant that examples have no strength when the question is of law. As if I should ask, what marriage is lawful; and it should be answered that lawful it is to man not only to have many wives at once, but also it is lawful to marry two sisters and to enjoy them, both living at once, because that David, Jacob, and Solomon, servants of God, did the same, I trust that no man would justify the vanity of this reason. Or if the question were demanded if a Christian with good conscience may defraud, steal, or deceive, and answer were made that so he might by the example of the Israelites, who at God's commandment deceived the Egyptians and spoiled them of their garments, gold, and silver, I think likewise this reason should be mocked. And what greater force, I pray you, hath the former argument? Deborah did rule in Israel, and Huldah spoke prophecy in Judah; *ergo*, it is lawful for women to reign above realms and nations or to teach in the presence of men. The consequent is vain and of none effect. For of examples, as is before declared, we may establish no law, but we are always bound to the law written and to the commandment expressed in the same. And the law written and pronounced by God forbiddeth no less that any women reign over man than it forbiddeth man to take plurality of wives, to marry two sisters living at once, to steal, to rob, to murder, or to lie. If any of these hath been transgressed, and yet God hath not imputed the same, it maketh not the like fact[72] or deed lawful unto us. For God, being free, may for such causes as be approved by his inscrutable wisdom dispense with the rigor of his law and may use his creatures at his pleasure. But the same power is not permitted to man, whom he hath made subject to his law and not to the examples of fathers. And this I think sufficient to the reasonable and moderate spirits.

But to repress the raging of woman's madness, I will descend somewhat deeper into the matter and not fear to affirm that, as we find a contrary spirit in all these most wicked women that this day be exalted into this tyrannous authority to the spirit that was in those godly matrons, so I fear not, I say, to affirm that their condition is unlike and that their end shall be diverse. In those matrons we find that the spirit of mercy, truth, justice, and of humility did reign. Under them we find that God did shew mercy to his people, delivering them from the tyranny of strangers and the venom of idolatry by the hands and counsel of those women; but in these our ages, we find cruelty, falsehood, pride, covetousness, deceit, and oppression. In them we also find the spirit of Jezebel and Athaliah; under them we find the simple people oppressed, the true religion extinguished, and the blood of Christ's members most cruelly shed. And finally, by their practices and deceit, we find ancient realms and nations given and betrayed into the hands of stranger, the titles and liberties of them taken from the just possessors. Which one thing is an evident testimony how unlike our mischievous Maries be unto Deborah, under whom were strangers chased out of Israel, God so raising her up to be a mother and deliverer to his oppressed people. But, alas, he hath raised up these Jezebels to be the uttermost of his plagues, the which man's unthankfulness hath long deserved. But his secret and most just judgment shall neither excuse them, neither their retainers, because their counsels be diverse.

But to prosecute my purpose, let such as list to defend these monsters in their tyranny prove first, that their sovereign mistresses be like to Deborah in godliness and pity, and secondarily, that the same success doth follow their tyranny which did follow the extraordinary regiment of that godly matron. Which thing, although they were able to do (as they never shall be, let them blow till they burst), yet shall her example profit them nothing at all. For they are never able to prove that either Deborah, or any other godly woman, having the commendation of the Holy Ghost within the Scriptures, hath usurped authority above any realm or nation by reason of their birth and blood. Neither yet did they claim it by right or inheritance. But God, by his singular privilege, favor, and grace, exempted Deborah from the common malediction given to women in that behalf; and against nature he made her prudent in counsel, strong in courage, happy in regiment, and a blessed mother and deliverer to his people. The which he did partly to advance and notify the power of his majesty, as well to his enemies, as to his own people. In that he declared himself able to give salvation and deliverance by means of the most weak vessels, and partly he did it to confound and ashame all men of that age, because they had for the most part declined from his true obedience. And therefore was the spirit of courage, regiment, and boldness taken from them for a time to their confusion and further humiliation. But what maketh this for Mary and her match Philip?

One thing I would ask of such as depend upon the example of Deborah: whether she was widow or wife when she judged Israel and when that God gave that notable victory to his people under her? If they answer she was widow, I would lay against them the testimony of the Holy Ghost, witnessing that she was wife to Lapidoth.[73] And if they will shift and allege that so she might be called, notwithstanding that her husband was dead, I urge them further that they are not able to prove it to be any common phrase and manner of speech in the Scriptures that a woman shall be called the wife of a dead man, except that there be some note added whereby it may be known that her husband is departed, as is witnessed of Anna.[74] But in this place of the Judges there is no note added that her husband should be dead, but rather the expressed contrary. For the text saith, "In that time a woman named Deborah, a prophetess, wife to Lapidoth, judged Israel."[75] The Holy Ghost plainly speaketh that what time she judged Israel, she was wife to Lapidoth.

If she was wife, and if she ruled all alone in Israel, then, I ask, why did she not prefer her husband to that honor to be captain and to be leader in the host of the Lord? For it affirmeth that Barak of the tribe of Naphtali was appointed to that office. If Barak had been her husband, to what purpose should the Holy Ghost so diligently have noted the tribe and another name than was before expressed? Yea, to what purpose should it be noted that she send and call him? Whereof I doubt not but that every reasonable man doth consider that this Barak was not her husband; and thereof, likewise, it is evident that her judgment or government in Israel was no such usurped power as our queens unjustly possess this day, but that it was the spirit of prophecy which rested upon her what time the multitude of people had wrought wickedly in the eyes of the Lord. By the which spirit she did rebuke the idolatry and iniquity of the people, exhort them to repentance, and, in the end, did bring them this comfort, that God should deliver them from the bondage and thralldom of their enemies. And this she might do, notwithstanding that another did occupy the place of the supreme magistrate (if any was in those days in Israel). For so I find did Huldah the wife of Shallum in the days of Josiah, King of Judah, speak prophecy and comfort the king; and yet he resigned to her neither the scepter nor the sword.[76] That this is our true interpretation: how that Deborah did judge in Israel is the true meaning of the Holy Ghost, the pondering and weighing of the history shall manifestly prove.

When she sendeth for Barak, I pray you, in whose name giveth she him his charge? Doth she speak to him as kings and princes use to speak to their subjects in such cases? No, but she speaketh as she that had a special revelation from God, which neither was known to Barak nor to the people, saying, "Hath not the Lord God of Israel commanded thee?" This is her preface by the which she would stir up the dull senses of Barak and of the people, willing to persuade unto them that the time was comen when God would shew himself their protector and deliverer; in which preface she usurpeth to herself neither power nor authority. For she saith not, "I, being thy princess, thy mistress, thy sovereign lady and queen, command thee upon thine allegiance, and under pain of treason, to go and gather an army." No, she spoileth herself of all power to command, attributing that authority to God of whom she had her revelation and certitude to appoint Barak captain, which after appeareth more plainly. For when she had declared to him the whole counsel of God, appointing unto him as well the number of soldiers, as the tribes out of which they should be gathered, and when she had appointed the place of the battle (which she could not have done, but by especial revelation of God), and had assured him of victory in the name of God, and yet that he fainted and openly refused to enter into that journey except that the prophetess would accompany him, she did use against him no external power; she did not threaten him with rebellion and death. But for assurance of his faint heart and weak conscience, being content to go with him, she pronounceth that the glory should not be his in that journey, but that the Lord should sell Sisera into the hand of a woman.[77] Such as have more pleasure in light than in darkness may clearly perceive that Deborah did usurp no such power nor authority as our queens do this day claim.

But that she was indued with the spirit of wisdom, of knowledge, and of the true fear of God, and by the same she judged facts of the rest of the people. She rebuked their defection and idolatry, yea, and also did redress to her power the injuries that were done by man to man. But all this, I say, she did by the spiritual sword, that is, by the word of God, and not by any temporal regiment or authority which she did usurp over Israel, in which, I suppose, at that time there was no lawful magistrate by the reason of their great affliction. For so witnesseth the history, saying, "And Ehud being dead, the Lord sold Israel into the hand of Jabin, King of Canaan."[78] And he, by Sisera his captain afflicted Israel greatly the space of twenty years. And Deborah herself, in her song of thanksgiving, confesseth that before she did arise mother in Israel, and in the days of Jael, there was nothing but confusion and trouble.

If any stick to the term, alleging that the Holy Ghost saith that she judged Israel, let them understand that neither doth the Hebrew word, neither yet the Latin, always signify civil judgment or the execution of the temporal sword, but most commonly is taken in the sense which we have before expressed. For of Christ it is said, "He shall judge nations."[79] And that, "He shall pronounce judgment to the gentiles."[80] And yet it is evident that he was no minister of the temporal sword. God commandeth Jerusalem and Judah to judge betwixt him and his vineyard, and yet he appointed not them all to be civil magistrates.[81] To Ezekiel it is said, "Shalt not thou judge them, son of man?" and after, "Thou son of man, shalt thou not judge? Shalt thou not judge, I say, the city of blood?" and also, "Behold I shall judge betwixt man and beast."[82] And such places in great number are to be found throughout the Holy Scriptures, and yet, I trust no man will be so foolish as to think that any of the prophets were appointed by God to be politic judges or to punish the sins of man by corporal punishment. No, the manner of their judgment is expressed in these words: "Declare to them all their abominations, and thou shalt say to them: Thus saith the Lord God, a city shedding blood in the mist of her, that her time may approach and which hath made idols against herself that she might be polluted. Thou hast transgressed in the blood which thou hast shed, and thou art polluted in the idols which thou hast made."[83] Thus, I say, do the prophets of God judge, pronouncing the sentence of God against malefactors.

And so I doubt not but Deborah judged, what time Israel had

declined from God, rebuking their defection and exhorting them to repentance, without usurpation of any civil authority. And if the people gave unto her for a time any reverence or honor, as her godliness and happy counsel did well deserve, yet was it no such empire as our monsters claim. For which of her sons or nearest kinsmen left she ruler and judge in Israel after her? The Holy Ghost expresseth no such thing. Whereof it is evident that by her example God offereth no occasion to establish any regiment of women above men, realms, and nations.

But now to the second objection in which women require, as to them appeareth, nothing but equity and justice, whilst they and their patrons for them require dominion and empire above men. For this is their question: Is it not lawful that women have their rights and inheritance, like as the daughters of Zelophehad were commanded by the mouth of Moses to have their portion of ground in their tribe?

I answer it is not only lawful that women possess their inheritance, but I affirm also that justice and equity require that so they do. But therewith I add that which gladly they list not understand: that to bear rule or authority over man can never be right nor inheritance to woman. For that can neither be just inheritance to any person which God by his word hath plainly denied unto them, but to all women hath God denied authority above man, as most manifestly is before declared. Therefore, to her it can never be inheritance, and thus must the advocates of our ladies provide some better example and stronger argument. For the law made in favor of the daughters of Zelophehad will serve them nothing. And assuredly great wonder it is that in so great light of God's truth men list to grope and wander in darkness. For let them speak of conscience, if the petition of any of these forenamed women was to reign over any one tribe, yea, or yet over any one man within Israel. Plain it is, they did not, but only required that they might have a portion of ground among the men of their tribe, lest the name of their father should be abolished. And this was granted unto them without respect had to any civil regiment. And what maketh this, I pray you, for the establishing of this monstrous empire of women? The question is not if women may not succeed to possession, substance, patrimony, or inheritance, such as fathers may leave to their children; for that I willingly grant. But the question is if women may succeed to their fathers in offices, and chiefly to that office the executor whereof doth occupy the place and throne of God. And that I absolutely deny, and fear not to say that to place a woman in authority above a realm is to pollute and profane the royal seat, the throne of justice, which ought to be the throne of God; and that to maintain them in the same is nothing else but continually to rebel against God.

One thing is yet to be noted and observed in the law made concerning the inheritance of the daughters of Zelophehad, to wit, that it was forbidden unto them to marry without their own tribe, lest that such portion as fell to their lot should be transferred from one tribe to another and so should the tribe of Manasseh be defrauded and spoiled of their just inheritance by their occasion. For avoiding of which, it was commanded by Moses that they should marry in the family or household of the tribe and kindred of their father.[84, 85]

Wonder it is that the advocates and patrons of the right of our ladies did not consider and ponder this law before that they counseled the blind princes and unworthy nobles of their countries to betray the liberties thereof into the hands of strangers. England, for satisfying of the inordinate appetites of that cruel monster Mary (unworthy by reason of her bloody tyranny of the name of a woman), betrayed, alas, to the proud Spaniard; and Scotland, by the rash madness of foolish governors and by the practices of a crafty dame, resigned likewise, under title of marriage, into the power of France.

Doth such translation of realms and nations please the justice of God, or is the possession, by such means obtained, lawful in his sight? Assured I am that it is not. No otherwise, I say, than is that possession whereunto thieves, murderers, tyrants, and oppressors do attain by theft, murder, tyranny, violence, deceit, and oppression—which God of his secret, but yet most just, judgment doth often permit for punishment as well of the sufferers as of the violent oppressors, but doth never approve the same as lawful and godly. For if he would not permit that the inheritance of the children of Israel should pass from one tribe to another by the marriage of any daughter (notwithstanding that they were all one people, all spake one tongue, all were descended of one father, and all did profess one God and one religion), if yet, I say, God would not suffer that the commodity and usual fruit which might be gathered of the portion of the ground limited and assigned to one tribe should pass to another, will he suffer that the liberties, laws, commodities, and fruits of whole realms and nations be given into the power and distribution of others by the reason of marriage and in the powers of such as, besides that they be of strange tongue, of strange manners and laws, they are also ignorant of God, enemies to his truth, deniers of Christ Jesus, persecutors of his true members, and haters of all virtue? As the odious nation of Spaniards doth manifestly declare, who for very despite which they do bear against Christ Jesus, whom their forefathers did crucify (for Jews they are, as histories do witness and they themselves confess) do this day make plain war against all true professors of his Holy Gospel.[86] And how blindly and outrageously the French King and his pestilent prelates do fight against the verity of God, the flaming fires which lick up the innocent blood of Christ's members do witness, and by his cruel edicts is notified and proclaimed.[87] And yet to these two cruel tyrants—to France and Spain, I mean—is the right and possession of England and Scotland appointed.

But just or lawful shall that possession never be till God do change the statute of his former law, which he will not do for the pleasure of man.[88] For he hath not created the earth to satisfy the ambition of two or three tyrants, but for the universal seed of Adam; and hath appointed and defined the bounds of their habitation to diverse nations, assigning divers countries, as he himself confesseth speaking to Israel in these words: "You shall pass by the bounds and limits of your brethren the sons of Esau who dwell in Mount Seir. They shall fear you, but take diligent heed that ye shew not yourselves cruel against them. For I will give you no part of their land, no, not the breadth of a foot, for Mount Seir I have given to Esau to be possessed."[89] And the same he doth witness of the sons of Lot, to whom he had given Ar to be possessed.[90] And Moses plainly affirmeth that when the Almighty did distribute and divide possessions to the gentiles, and when he did disperse and scatter the sons of men, that then he did appoint the limits and bounds of peoples for the number of the sons of Israel. Whereof it is plain that God hath not exposed the earth in prey to tyrants, making all things lawful which by violence and murder they may possess; but that he hath appointed to every several nation a several possession, willing them to stand content (as nature did teach an ethnic[91] to affirm) with that portion which by lot and just means they had enjoyed.[92] For what causes God permitteth this distribution to be troubled and the realms of ancient nations to be possessed of strangers, I delay at this time to entreat. Only this I have recited to give the world to understand that the reign, empire, and authority of women hath no ground within God's Scriptures. Yea, that realms or provinces possessed by their marriage is nothing but unjust conquest. For so little doth the law made for the daughters of Zelophehad help the cause of your queens that utterly it fighteth against them, both damning their authority and fact. But now to the third objection.

The consent, say they, of realms and laws pronounced admitted in this behalf, long consuetude and custom, together with the felicity of some women in their empires, have established their authority. To whom, I answer, that neither may the tyranny of princes, neither the foolishness of people, neither wicked laws made against God, neither yet the felicity that in this earth hereof may ensue, make that thing lawful which he by his word hath manifestly condemned. For if the approbation of princes and people, laws made by men, or the consent of realms may establish anything against God and his word, then should idolatry be preferred to the true religion. For more realms and nations, more laws and decrees published by emperors with common consent of their councils, have established the one than have approved the other. And yet I think that no man of sound judgment will therefore justify and defend idolatry. No more ought any man to maintain this odious empire of women, although that it were approved all men by their laws. For the same God that in plain words forbiddeth idolatry doth also forbid the authority of women over man, as the words of St. Paul before rehearsed do plainly teach us. And therefore, whether women be deposed from that unjust authority—have they never usurped it so long—or if all such honor be denied unto them, I fear not to affirm that they are neither defrauded of right nor inheritance. For to women can that honor never be due nor lawful—much less inheritance—which God hath so manifestly denied unto them.

I am not ignorant that the subtle wits of carnal men (which can never be brought under the obedience of God's simple precepts to maintain this monstrous empire) have yet two vain shifts. First they allege that albeit women may not absolutely reign by themselves, because they may neither sit in judgment, neither pronounce sentence, neither execute any public office; yet may they do all such things by their lieutenants, deputies, and judges substitute. Secondarily, say they, a woman born to rule over any realm may choose her a husband and to him she may transfer and give her authority and right. To both I answer in few words. First, that from a corrupt and venomed fountain can spring no wholesome water. Secondarily, that no person hath power to give the thing which doth not justly appertain to themselves.

But the authority of a woman is a corrupted fountain, and therefore from her can never spring any lawful officer. She is not born to rule over men, and therefore she can appoint none by her gift nor by her power, which she hath not, to the place of a lawful magistrate.[93] And therefore whosoever receiveth of a woman office or authority are adulterous and bastard officers before God. This may appear strange at the first affirmation, but if we will be as indifferent and equal in the cause of God as that we can be in the cause of man, the reason shall suddenly appear. The case supposed that a tyrant by conspiracy usurped the royal seat and dignity of a king, and in the same did so establish himself that he appointed officers and did what him list for a time; and in this meantime the native king made strait inhibition to all his subjects that none should adhere to this traitor, neither yet receive any dignity of him; yet, nevertheless, they would honor the same traitor as king and become his officers in all affairs of the realm. If, after the native prince did recover his just honor and possession, should he repute or esteem any man of the traitor's appointment for a lawful magistrate or for his friend and true subject? Or should he not rather with one sentence condemn the head with the members? And if so he should do, who were able to accuse him of rigor, much less to condemn his sentence of injustice? And dare we deny the same power to God in the like case? For that woman reigneth above man, she hath obtained it by treason and conspiracy committed against God. How can it be then that she, being guilty of treason against God committed, can appoint any officer pleasing in his sight? It is a thing impossible.

Wherefore, let men that receive of women authority, honor, or office be most assuredly persuaded that in so maintaining that usurped power they declare themselves enemies to God. If any think that because the realm and estates thereof have given their consents to a woman and have established her and her authority, that therefore it is lawful and acceptable before God, let the same men remember what I have said before, to wit, that God cannot approve the doing nor consent of any multitude concluding anything against his word and ordinance, and therefore they must have a more assured defense against the wrath of God than the approbation and consent of a blinded multitude, or else they shall not be able to stand in the presence of the consuming fire; that is, they must acknowledge that the regiment of a woman is a thing most odious in the presence of God. They must refuse to be her officers, because she is a traitoress and rebel against God. And finally, they must study to repress her inordinate pride and tyranny to the uttermost of their power.

The same is the duty of the nobility and estates, by whose blindness a woman is promoted. First, insofar as they have most heinously offended against God, placing in authority such as by his word hath removed from the same, unfeignedly they ought to call for mercy; and, being admonished of their error and damnable fact, in sign and token of true repentance, with common consent they ought to retreat that which unadvisedly and by ignorance they have pronounced, and ought without further delay to remove from authority all such persons as by usurpation, violence, or tyranny do possess the same. For so did Israel and Judah after they had revolted from David, and Judah alone in the days of Athaliah. For after that she, by murdering her son's children, had obtained the empire over the land and had most unhappily reigned in Judah six years, Jehoiada, the high priest, called together the captains and chief rulers of the people, shewing to them the king's son Joash, did bind them by an oath to depose that wicked woman and to promote the king to his royal seat, which they faithfully did, killing at his commandment not only that cruel and mischievous woman, but also the people did destroy the temple of Baal, break his altars and images, and kill Mattan, Baal's high priest before his altars.[94]

The same is the duty as well of the estates as of the people that hath been blinded. First, they ought to remove from honor and authority that monster against nature (so call I a woman clad in the habit of man, yea, a woman against nature reigning above man). Secondarily, if any presume to defend that impiety, they ought not to fear, first, to pronounce and then after to execute the sentence of death. If any man be afraid to violate the oath of obedience which they have made to such monsters, let them be most assuredly persuaded that, as the beginning of their oaths, proceeding from ignorance, was sin, so is the obstinate purpose to keep the same nothing but plain rebellion against God. But of this matter in *The Second Blast*, God willing, we shall speak more at large.[95]

And now to put an end to *The First Blast*, seeing that by the order of nature, by the malediction and curse pronounced against woman by the mouth of St. Paul, the interpreter of God's sentence, by the example of that commonwealth in which God by his word planted order and policy, and finally, by the judgment of the most godly writers, God hath dejected woman from rule, dominion, empire, and authority above man. Moreover, seeing that neither the example of Deborah, neither the law made for the daughters of Zelophehad, neither yet the foolish consent of an ignorant multitude, be able to justify that which God so plainly hath condemned, let all men take heed what quarrel and cause from henceforth they do defend.

If God raise up any noble heart to vindicate the liberty of his country and to suppress the monstrous empire of women, let all such as shall presume to defend them in the same most certainly know that in so doing they lift their hand against God, and that one day they shall find his power to fight against their foolishness. Let not the faithful, godly, and valiant hearts of Christ's soldiers be utterly discouraged, neither yet let the tyrants rejoice, albeit for a time they triumph against such as study to repress their tyranny and to remove them from unjust authority. For the causes alone, why he suffereth the soldiers to fail in battle, whom, nevertheless, he commandeth to fight, as sometimes did Israel fighting against Benjamin.

The cause of the Israelites was most just; for it was to punish that horrible abomination of those sons of Belial—abusing the Levite's wife—whom the Benjamites did defend. And they had God's precept to assure them of well-doing. For he did not only command them to fight, but also appointed Judah to be their leader and captain, and yet fell they twice in plain battle against those most wicked adulterers. The secret cause of this, I say, is known to God alone. But by his evident Scriptures we may assuredly gather that by such means doth his wisdom sometimes beat down the pride of the flesh, for the Israelites at the first trusted in their multitude, power, and strength. And sometimes by such overthrows he will punish the offenses of his own children and bring them to the unfeigned knowledge of the same before he will give them victory against the manifest contemners, whom he hath appointed, nevertheless, to uttermost perdition, as the end of that battle did witness. For although with great murder the children of Israel did twice fall before the Benjamites, yet after they had wept before the Lord, after they had fasted and made sacrifice in sign of their unfeigned repentance, they so prevailed against that proud tribe of Benjamin that, after 25,000 strong men of war were killed in battle, they destroyed man, woman, child, and beast, as well in the fields as in the cities, which all were burned with fire so that only of that whole tribe remained six hundred men, who fled to the wilderness, where they remained four months and so were saved.[96]

The same God who did execute this grievous punishment, even by those whom he suffered twice to be overcomen in battle, doth this day retain his power and justice. Cursed Jezebel of England, with the pestilent and detestable generation of papists, make no little brag and boast that they have triumphed not only against Wyatt, but also against all such as have enterprised anything against them or their proceedings.[97] But let her and them consider that yet they have not prevailed against God; his throne is more high than the length of their horns be able to reach. And let them further consider that in the beginning of this their bloody reign the harvest of their iniquity was not comen to full maturity and ripeness. No, it was so green, so secret I mean, so covered, and so hid with hypocrisy that some men—even the servants of God— thought it not impossible but that wolves might be changed into lambs, and also that the viper might remove her natural venom. But God, who doth reveal in his time appointed the secrets of hearts and that will have his judgments justified even by the very wicked, hath now given open testimony of her and their beastly cruelty. For man and woman, learned and unlearned, nobles and men of baser sort, aged fathers and tender damsels, and finally the bones of the dead, as well women as men, have tasted of their tyranny. So that now not only the blood of father Latimer, of the mild man of God, the bishop of Canterbury, of learned and discrete Ridley, of innocent Lady Jane Dudley,[98] and many godly and worthy preachers that cannot be forgotten, such as fire hath consumed and the sword of tyranny most unjustly hath shed, doth call for vengeance in the ears of the Lord God of hosts; but also the sobs and tears of the oppressed, the groanings of the angels, the watchmen of the Lord, yea, and every earthly creature abused by their tyranny, do continually cry and call for the hasty execution of the same.

I fear not to say that the day of vengeance, which shall apprehend that horrible monster Jezebel of England and such as maintain her monstrous cruelty, is already appointed in the counsel of the Eternal; and I verily believe that it is so nigh that she shall not reign so long in tyranny as hitherto she hath done, when God shall declare himself to be her enemy, when he shall pour forth contempt upon her according to her cruelty, and shall kindle the hearts of such as sometimes did favor her with deadly hatred against her, that they may execute his judgments. And therefore let such as assist her take heed what they do. For assuredly her empire and reign is a wall without foundation; I mean the same of the authority of all women. It hath been underpropped this blind time that is past with the foolishness of people and the wicked laws of ignorant and tyrannous princes. But the fire of God's word is already laid to those rotten props (I include the Pope's law with the rest), and presently they burn, albeit we espy not the flame. When they are consumed (as shortly they will be, for stubble and dry timber cannot long endure the fire), that rotten wall—the usurped and unjust empire of women—shall fall by itself in despite of all man, to the destruction of so many as shall labor to uphold it. And therefore let all man be advertised, for the trumpet hath once blown.

Praise God, ye that fear him.

Notes

1. 1 Kings 12.
2. Ezek. 16.
3. Jer. 29.
4. Ezek. 7, 8, 9.
5. Isa. 13; Jer. 46; Ezek. 36.
6. Ezek. 2.
7. Rev. 16.
8. 1 Cor. 9:16.
9. Matt. 26; Acts 18, 21.
10. Ps. 2; Acts 4.
11. [supporters]
12. 2 Kings 6.
13. Matt. 14. [Luke 32.]
14. Rom. 1
15. Ezek. 33:7, 8, 9.
16. [Knox only published an outline of *The Second Blast;* there was no third.]
17. Aristotle *Politics* 2.1269b9.
18. Justin Martyr *Discourse to the Greeks* 1.
19. Aristotle *Politics* 1270a13.
20. *Dig.* 50.17.2 (*de diversis regulis iuris antiqui*).
21. *Dig.* 3.1.1 (*de postulando*).
22. *Dig.* 16.1.pr. (*ad senatus consultum velleiandum*).
23. *Dig.* 3.1.pr. (*de postulando*) and *Dig.* 16.1.pr. *Dig.* 16.1.8.
24. *Dig.* 1.5.9. (*de statu hominum*).
25. *Dig.* 3.1.1. and *Inst.* 1.1.11. (*de adopt*).
26. The passage is obliquely referred to in *Dig.* 3.1. (*de postulando*).
27. England and Scotland beware.
28. 2 Kings 11.

29. 1 Cor. 11:8, 9, 10.
30. Gen. 3:16.
31. Ibid.
32. 1 Tim. 2:12.
33. 1 Cor. 14:34.
34. Tertullian *De Habitu Muliebri* i.1.2.
35. Tertullian *De Virginibus Velandis* 9.
36. Tertullian *Contra Marcionem* i.1.
37. Augustine *Contra Faustum Manichaeum* xxii.31.
38. Augustine *De Trinitate* xii.7.10.
39. Ibid.
40. Augustine *De Continentia* 9.23.
41. Ambrose *Hexameron* v.7.
42. Ambrose *Of the Christian Faith* iv.28.32; and *Paradise* iv.24.
43. Ambrose *Paradise* 10.48.
44. Ambrose *De Helia Ieiunio* 18.16.
45. Whose house, I pray you, ought the parliament house to be, God's or the devil's?
46. Knox cited Chrysostom *Homilies on Genesis* 17. The quotation was not located in Chrysostom.
47. Chrysostom *Homilies on Genesis* 17.
48. Chrysostom *Homilies on Genesis* 15.
49. Chrysostom *Homilies on the Ephesians* 13.
50. Chrysostom *Homilies on St. John* 87. [The reference is not to woman in general but prostitutes in particular.]
51. Ibid.
52. Basil *The Morals* 73.6 [I Tim. 1.]
53. Augustine *De Ordine* i.10.28.
54. Augustine *De civitate Dei* xix.13.
55. Ps. 115:5, 6, 7.
56. 1 Cor. 11:3.
57. Chrysostom *Homilies on First Corinthians* 26.
58. Rom. 1.
59. [Knox apparently meant the opportunities under Edward VI.]
60. [polity]
61. Deut. 17:14, 15.
62. Josh. 1:6, 7, 8.
63. Deut. 17:18, 19.
64. Gen. 4.
65. Matt. 27.
66. Acts 12:23.
67. 1 Tim. 2:12.
68. [To bear authority, to reign.]
69. Rev. 2.
70. Judg. 4; 2 Chron. 34.
71. Num. 27.
72. [act]
73. Judg. 4.
74. Luke 2.
75. Judg. 4:4.
76. 2 Kings 22.

77. [Judg. 4.]
78. [Judg. 4:2.]
79. Isa. 2:4.
80. Isa. 42:1.
81. Isa. 5.
82. Ezek. 20:4; 22:2; 34:17.
83. Ezek. 22:2, 3, 4.
84. Num. 36.
85. The Spaniards are Jews, and they brag that Mary of England is of the root of Jesse.
86. [Knox here called the Spaniards infidels. In the early 1620s Thomas Scot, the Puritan propagandist, added a racial note when he said that the Spaniards were really Moors.]
87. Note the law which he hath proclaimed in France against such as he termeth Lutherans. [In December 1557, Knox had written a translation with his addition of *An Apology for the Protestants Who Are Holden in Prison in Paris*. See Knox, *Works*, vol. 4 289–347.]
88. Knox cited Acts 17, but see Num. 36.
89. Deut. 2:4, 5.
90. Deut. 2:18, 19.
91. [heathen]
92. Cicero *De Officiis* 1.7, 21.
93. Let England and Scotland take heed.
94. 2 Kings 11.
95. [*The Second Blast* appeared only as a brief outline.]
96. Judg. 20.
97. [Sir Thomas Wyatt, whose rebellion against Mary failed in January 1554.]
98. [Hugh Latimer, Bishop of Worcester, and Nicholas Ridley, Bishop of London, were burned at the stake 16 October 1555; Thomas Cranmer, Archbishop of Canterbury, was burned 21 March 1556. Knox showed more sympathy to Cranmer dead than he had to Cranmer alive. Lady Jane Dudley (Grey) was executed 12 February 1554, in the aftermath of Wyatt's rebellion.]

2
Letter to the Regent of Scotland (1558)

The copy of a letter delivered to the Lady Mary, Regent of Scotland, from John Knox, minister of God's word, in the year of our Lord 1556, and now augmented and explained by the author in the year of our Lord 1558.

To the Excellent Lady Mary, Dowager Regent of Scotland.

The cause moving me, Right Honorable, to present this my supplication unto your Grace, enlarged and in some places explained (which, being in the realm of Scotland in the month of May 1556, I caused to be presented to your Grace), is the incredible rage of such as bear the title of bishops, who, against all justice and equity, have pronounced against me a most cruel sentence, condemning my body to fire, my soul to damnation, and all doctrine taught by me to be false, deceivable, and heretical.[1] If this injury did tend to me alone, having the testimony of a good conscience, with silence I could pass the matter, being assured that such as they curse and expel in their synagogues for such causes shall God bless and Christ Jesus receive in his eternal society. But considering that this their blasphemy is vomited forth against the eternal truth of Christ's Evangel—whereof it hath pleased the great mercy of God to make me a minister, I cannot cease to notify, as well to your Grace as unto them, that so little I am afraid of their tyrannical and surmised sentence that in the place of the picture, if God impede not my purpose, they shall have the body to justify that doctrine which they, members of Satan, blasphemously do condemn. Advertising your Grace in the meantime that from them, their sentence, and tyranny and from all those that list maintain them in the same, I do appeal to a lawful and general council; beseeching your Grace to take in good part that I call you for witness that I have required the liberty of tongue and my cause to be heard before your Grace and the body of that realm before that any such process was laid against me, as this my letter directed to your Grace doth testify.

The Beginning of the Letter.

The eternal providence of the same God who hath appointed his chosen children to fight in this transitory and wretched life a battle strong and difficile hath also appointed their final victory by a marvelous fashion and the manner of their preservation in their battle more marvelous.[2] Their victory standeth not in resisting but in suffering; as our sovereign master pronounceth to his disciples, that in their patience should they possess their souls.[3] And the same foresaw the Prophet Isaiah when that he painteth forth all other battle to be with violence, tumult, and bloodshedding, but the victory of God's people to be in quietness, silence, and hope, meaning that all others that obtain victory do enforce themselves to resist their adversaries, to shed blood, and to murder.[4] But so do not the elect of God, but all things they sustain at the commandment of him who hath appointed them to suffer, being most assuredly persuaded that then only they triumph when all men judge them oppressed. For in the cross of Christ always is included a secret and hid victory, never well known till the sufferer appear altogether to be, as it were, exterminate. For then only did the blood of Abel cry to God when proud Cain judged all memory of his brother to have been extinguished. And so I say their victory is marvelous.

And how that they can be preserved and not brought to utter confusion, the eye of man perceiveth not. But he, whose power is infinite, by secret and hid motions toucheth the hearts of such as, to man's judgment, have power to destroy them, of very pity and compassion to save his people: as that he did the hearts of the Egyptian midwives to preserve the men children of the Israelites when precept was given by Pharaoh of their destruction, the heart of Pharaoh's daughter likewise to pity Moses in his young infancy, exposed to the danger of the waters; the heart of Nebuchadnezzar to preserve the captives alive and liberally to nourish the children that were found apt to letters, and finally, the heart of Cyrus to set at liberty the people of God after long bondage and thralldom.[5] And thus doth the invisible power and love of God manifest itself toward his elect from time to time for two causes specially: first, to comfort his weak warriors in their manifold temptations, letting them understand that he is able to compel such as sometimes were enemies to his people to fight in their cause and to promote their deliverance; and secondarily, to give a testimony of his favor to them that by all appearance did live before, as St. Paul speaketh, wanting God in the world, as strangers from the commonwealth of Israel, and without the league of his merciful promise and free grace made to his church.[6] For who could have affirmed that any of these persons aforenamed had been of that nature and clemency before occasions were offered unto them? But the works of mercy shewed to the afflicted have left us assurance that God used them as vessels of his honor. For pity and mercy shewed to Christ's afflicted flock, as they never lacked reward temporal, so, if they be continued and be not changed into cruelty, are assured signs and seals of everlasting mercy to be received from God, who by his Holy Spirit moveth their hearts to shew mercy to the people of God oppressed and afflicted.

Addition

This preface I used to give your Grace occasion more deeply to consider what hath been the condition of Christ's members from the beginning that, in so doing, ye might see that it is no new thing that the saints of God be oppressed in the world, that ye, moved by earnest contemplation of the same, might also study rather to save them from murder (although by the wicked counsel of many ye were provoked to the contrary) than to be a slave to Satan, obeying his servants, your clergy, whose fury is bent against God and his verity. But this will after follow in our letter, which thus proceedeth.

Letter

Your Grace perchance doth wonder to what purpose these things be recited, and I in very deed cannot wonder enough that occasion is offered to me, a worm most wretched, to recite the same at this present. For I have looked rather for the sentence of death than to have written to your Grace in these last and most wicked days, in which Satan so blindeth the hearts of many that innocents are damned, their cause never tried.

Addition

Hereof ye cannot be ignorant. For besides these whom ye hear from time to time most cruelly to be murdered in France, Italy, Spain, Flanders, and now of late years beside you in England (for no cause but that they profess Christ Jesus to be the only savior of the world, the only mediator betwixt God and man, the only sacrifice acceptable for the sins of all faithful, and finally, the only head to his church),[7] besides these, I say, of whom ye hear the bruit, ye have been witness that some within the realm of Scotland for the same cause most cruelly have been murdered, whose cause was never heard with indifferency. But murderers, occupying the seat of justice, have shed the blood of Christ's true witnesses, which, albeit did then appear to be consumed away with fire, yet is it recent in the presence of him for whose cause they did suffer, and ceaseth not to call for vengeance with the blood of Abel, to fall not only upon such as were authors of that murder, but also upon all those that maintain those tyrants in their tyranny or that do consent to their beastly cruelty. Take not this as affirmation of any man, but hear and consider the voice of the son of God: "Fulfill," saith he, "that all the blood which hath been shed since the blood of Abel the just, till the blood of Zechariah," etc. "may come upon this generation."[8] Hereby it is evident that the murderers of our time as well in the time of Christ are guilty of all blood that hath been shed from the beginning.

Fearful, I grant is the sentence, yet is it most equal and just. For whosoever sheddeth the blood of any one of Christ Jesus his members for professing his truth, consenteth to all the murder which hath been made since the beginning of the world for that cause. So that as there is one communion of all God's elect, of whom every member is participant of the whole justice of Christ, so is there a communion among the reprobate, by which every one of the serpent's seed are criminal and guilty of all iniquity which the whole body committeth, for because they are all together conjured against Christ Jesus and against his eternal verity—every one serving Satan, the prince of the world, in their rank, age, degree, and estate. The murderers of their brethren which this day live are guilty with Cain of the blood of Abel.[9] The kings and princes, which by power oppress the people of God and will not suffer that the people truly worship God as he hath commanded but will retain them in Egypt, are brethren and companions to Pharaoh. The prelates and priests, whose horrible iniquities and insolent life have infected all realms where they reign, have with their fathers, the old Pharisees, taken away the key of knowledge and have shut up the kingdom of heaven before men, so that neither they themselves will enter, neither yet will they suffer others to enter the same.[10] And the multitude, blinded, some by ignorance, some by fear, and by insatiable appetite of their part of the spoil (for Christ

being crucified, the soldiers parted amongst them his garments),
are conjured to defend those murderers, proud pestilent prelates,
against Christ Jesus and against his poor flock; and therefore, because of one crime they are all guilty, which is of treason and
rebellion against Christ, of one torment they shall all taste, which
is of the fire that never shall be quenched. And herein ought you,
Madam, be circumspect and careful, if that ye have any hope of the
life to come. For if the consent which proceedeth of ignorance and
blindness bringeth destruction and death (as Christ, our master,
doth witness, saying, "If the blind lead the blind, they shall both
fall in the ditch"), what shall become of the proud and malicious
contemner of God's verity offered?[11]

But our doctrine, perchance, shall be denied to be the verity.
Whereunto I answer that so was the doctrine of Noah, of Moses,
of the Prophets, of Christ Jesus, and of his Apostles; and yet the
original world perished by water, Sodom and Gomorrah by fire
descending from heaven, Pharaoh and his adherents in the Red
Sea, the city of Jerusalem, the whole nation of the Jews by punishments and plagues, notwithstanding that the whole multitude
cried, "this is a new doctrine, this his heresy, and tendeth to sedition."[12] Our petition is that our doctrine may be tried by the plain
word of God, that liberty be granted to us to utter and declare our
minds at large in every article and point which now are in controversy; which, if ye deny, giving ear to Christ's enemies, who
condemn his doctrine for heresy, ye shall drink the cup of God's
vengeance with them. But now to the former letter.

Letter

I doubt not but the rumors which have comen to your Grace's
ears of me have been such that, if all reports were true, I were
unworthy to live in the earth; and wonder it is that the voices of
the multitude should not so have inflamed your Grace's heart with
just hatred of such a one as I am accused to be that all access to pity
should have been shut up. I am traduced as an heretic, accused as a
false teacher and seducer of the people, besides other opprobries
which, affirmed by men of worldly honor and estimation, may
easily kindle the wrath of magistrates where innocency is not
known. But blessed be God, the father of our Lord Jesus Christ,
who by the dew of his heavenly grace hath so quenched the fire of
displeasure as yet in your Grace's heart, which of late days I have
understand, that Satan is frustrate of his enterprise and purpose,
which is to my heart no small comfort.

Not so much, God is my witness, for any benefit that I can

receive in this miserable life by protection of any earthly creature (for the cup which it behooveth me to drink is appointed by the wisdom of him whose counsels are not changeable), as that I am for the benefit which, I am assured, your Grace shall receive, if that ye continue in like moderation and clemency towards others that most unjustly are and shall be accused as that your Grace hath begun towards me and my most desperate cause. That is, if that by godly wisdom ye shall study to bridle the fury and rage of them who, for the maintenance of their worldly pomp, regard nothing the cruel murdering of simple innocents, then shall he who doth pronounce mercy to appertain to the merciful and promiseth that a cup of cold water given for his name's sake shall not lack reward, first, cause your happy government to be praised in this present age and in posterities to come, and last, recompense your godly pains and study with that joy and glory which the eye hath not seen nor yet can enter into the heart of mortal creature.[13]

Addition

If Christ's words were esteemed true, that of every idle word an accompt shall be given, and that nothing is so secretly done which shall not come to knowledge and light, I suppose that the tongues of men shall be better bridled than impudently to speak their pleasure in matters unknown.[14] For albeit that the true fear of God should not move them to speak truth, yet would I think, if any spark of humanity remained, that worldly shame should impede them to lie. When reasoning was before your Grace what man it was that preached in Ayre, and divers men were of divers opinion, some affirming that it was an Englishman and some supposing the contrary, a prelate, not of the least pride, said, "Nay, no Englishman, but it is Knox that knave."[15] It was my lord's pleasure so to baptise a poor man. The reason whereof, if it should be required, his rochet and miter must stand for authority. What further liberty he used in defining things like uncertain to him, to wit, of my learning and doctrine, at this present I omit, lamenting more that such pestilent tongues have liberty to speak in the presence of princes than that I am sorry for any hurt that their venom can do to me in body or fame. For what hath my life and conversation been since it hath pleased God to call me from the puddle of papistry, let my very enemies speak. And what learning I have, they may prove when they please.

The report of your Grace's moderation, as well at that time as after, when suit was made for my apprehension, moved me to write this, my other letter, in which, albeit I have not played the orator, dilating and decking the matter for the pleasure of itching and delicate ears, yet doth my conscience bear me record that with simplicity I have advertised you of a mortal danger, as this portion subsequent shall prove.

Letter

Superfluous and foolish it shall appear to many that I, a man of base estate and condition, dare enterprise to admonish a princess so honorable, indued with wisdom and graces singular. But when I consider the honor which God commandeth to be given to magistrates which no doubt, if it be true honor, containeth in itself in lawful things obedience, and in all things love and reverence, when further I consider the troublesome estate of Christ's true religion this day oppressed by blindness of men, and last, the great multitude of flatterers and the rare number of them that boldly and plainly dare speak the naked verity in presence of their princes and principally in the cause of Christ Jesus, these things, I say, considered, whatsoever any man shall judge of my enterprise, I am compelled to say that, unless in your regiment and in using of power your Grace be found different from the multitude of princes and head rulers, that this pre-eminence wherein ye are placed shall be your dejection to torment and pain everlasting.[16] This proposition is sore; but, alas, it is so true that if I should conceal and hide it from your Grace, I committed no less treason against your Grace than if I did see you by imprudency take a cup, which I knew to be poisoned or invenomed, and yet would not admonish you to abstain from drinking of the same. The religion, which this day men defend by fire and sword, is a cup invenomed, of which whosoever drinketh—except that by true repentance he after drink of the water of life—drinketh therewith damnation and death.[17] How and by whom it hath been invenomed, if it were no more tedious to your Grace to read or hear than it is painful to me to write or rehearse, I would not spare the labor; but for this present I have thought it some discharge of one part of my duty, if I, of very love, admonish your Grace of the danger, which I do, as God one day shall declare, preferring your Grace's salvation and the salvation of the people, now committed to your charge, to any corporal benefit that can redound to myself.

Addition

As Satan by craft hath corrupted the most holy ordinances of God's precepts—I mean of the first table—in the place of the spiritual honoring of God, introducing men's dreams, inventions, and fantasies, so hath he, abusing the weakness of man, corrupted this precept of the second table, touching the honor which is due to parents, under whom are comprehended princes and teachers. For now the devil hath so blinded the senses of many that they cannot or, at the least, will not learn what appertaineth to God and what to Caesar. But because the Spirit of God hath said, "honor the king"; therefore, whatsoever they command, be it right or wrong, must be obeyed. But heavy shall the judgment be which shall apprehend such blasphemers of God's majesty who dare be so bold as to affirm that God hath commanded any creature to be obeyed against himself. Against God it is that for the command-ment of any prince, be he never so potent, men shall commit idolatry, embrace a religion which God hath not approved by his word, or confirm by their silence wicked and blasphemous laws made against the honor of his majesty. Men, I say, that so do give not true obedience; but, as they are apostates from God, so are they traitors to their princes, whom by flattery they confirm in rebelling against God.

Only they which to the death resist such wicked laws and de-crees are acceptable to God and faithful to their princes: as were the three children in the presence of Nebuchadnezzar and Daniel in the days of Darius, the Persian Emperor, whose constant and free confession, as it glorified God, so did it notify, as well as those tyrants as to all ages following, the great blasphemy which in their rage and fury they committed against God, from the which, by all appearance, neither of both so suddenly should have been called, if the three children had bowed amongst the rest, and Daniel had not declared the confession of his faith, which was with windows open to pray towards Jerusalem, manifestly thereby declaring that he did not consent to the blasphemous law and decree which was established by the King and his council.[18] Experience hath taught us what surmises and blasphemies the adversaries of Christ Jesus, of his eternal verity do invent and devise against such as begin to detect their impiety. They are accused to be authors of sedition, raisers of tumults, violators of common order, etc. I answer with the Prophet Isaiah, that, "all is not reputed before God sedition and conjuration which the foolish multitude so esteemeth," neither yet is every tumult and breach of public order contrary to God's commandment.[19] For Christ Jesus himself, coming to rive the spoil from the strong-armed, who before did keep his house in quietness, is not comen to send peace but a sword and to make a

man disassent from his father, etc.[20] His Prophets before him and
Apostles after him feared not to break public orders established
against God and, in so doing, to move, as it were, the one half of
peoples, nations, and cities against the other.[21] And yet I trust that
none except the hired servant of Satan will accuse Christ of sedition nor his Apostles of the troubling of commonwealths.

True it is that the most wholesome medicine most troubleth for a
time the body replenished with wicked and corrupted humors, but
the cause hereof is known to be not in the medicine but in the body
subject to malady; even so the true word of God, when it entereth
to fight where Satan hath borne dominion (as he still doth in the
whole papistry), cannot but appear to be occasion of great trouble.
But, Madam, more profitable it is that the pestilent humors be
expelled with pain than that they be nourished to the destruction
of the body. The papistical religion is a mortal pestilence which
shall assuredly bring to death eternal the bodies and souls from the
which it is not purged in this life.

And therefore take heed betimes; God calleth upon you; beware
that ye shut not up your ears. Judge not the matter after the vility
of my body, whom God hath appointed ambassador and messenger unto you, but with reverence and fear consider him whose
message I bear. I come to you in the name of the eternal God and
of Christ Jesus his son, to whom the father hath committed all
power, whom he hath established sovereign judge over all flesh,
before whose throne ye must make accompt with what reverence
ye hear such as he sendeth. It shall not excuse you to say or think
that ye doubt whether I be sent of God or no. I cry unto you that
the religion which the princes and blinded papists maintain with
fire and sword is not the religion of Christ, that your proud prelates are none of Christ's bishops. I admonish you that Christ's
flock is oppressed by them; and therefore I require, and that yet
again in the name of the Lord Jesus, that with indifferency I may
be heard to preach, to reason, and to dispute in that cause, which,
if ye deny, ye declare yourself to bear no reverence to Christ nor
love to his true religion.

Letter

But ye think, peradventure, that the care of religion is not committed to magistrates but to the bishops and estate ecclesiastical, as
they term it. But deceive not yourself. For the negligence of
bishops shall no less be required of the hands of magistrates than
shall the oppression of false judges. For they injustly promote,
foster, and maintain the one and the other. The false and corrupt

judge to spoil the goods and to oppress the bodies of the simple, but the proud prelates do kings maintain to murder the souls, for the which the blood of Christ Jesus was shed. And that they do either by withholding from them the true word of life, or else by causing teach unto them a pestilent doctrine such as now is taught in the papistical churches.

I know that ye wonder how that which is universally received can be so damnable and corrupted. But if your Grace shall consider that ever from the beginning the multitude hath declined from God[22] (yea, even in the people to whom he spake by his Law and Prophets),[23] if ye shall consider the complaint of the Holy Ghost, complaining that nations, people, princes, and kings of the earth have raged, made conspiracies, and holden counsels against the Lord and against his anointed Christ Jesus;[24] further, if ye shall consider the question which Jesus himself doth move in these words: "When the son of man shall come, shall he find faith in the earth?";[25] and last, if your Grace shall consider the manifest contempt of God and all his holy precepts which this day reign without punishment upon the face of the whole earth (for as Hosea complaineth, "there is no verity, there is no mercy, there is no truth this day among men; but lies, perjury, and oppression overflow all, and blood toucheth blood," that is, every iniquity is joined to another);[26] if deeply, I say, your Grace shall contemplate the universal corruption that this day reigneth in all estates, then shall your Grace cease to wonder that "many are called and few chosen."[27] And ye shall begin to tremble and fear to follow the multitude to perdition.[28] The universal defection, whereof St. Paul did prophesy, is easily to be espied, as well in religion as in manners.[29] The corruption of life is evident, and religion is not judged nor measured by the plain word of God, but by custom, consuetude, will, consent, and determination of men.

But shall he who hath pronounced all cogitations of man's heart to be vain at all times, accept the counsels and consents of men for a religion pleasing and acceptable before him? Let not your Grace be deceived. God cannot lie; God cannot deny himself. He hath witnessed from the beginning that no religion pleaseth him except that which he by his own word hath commanded and established.[30] The verity itself pronounceth this sentence: "In vain do they worship me, teaching doctrines the precepts of men," and also, "All plantations which my heavenly father hath not planted shall be rooted out."[31] Before the coming of his well-beloved son in flesh, severely he punished all such as durst enterprise to alter or change his ceremonies and statutes, as in Saul, Uzziah, Nadab, Abihu is to be read.[32] And will he know, after that he hath opened his counsel to the world by his only son whom he commandeth to be heard, and after by his Holy Spirit, speaking in his Apostles, he hath established the religion in which he will his true worshippers abide to the end, will he now, I say, admit men's inventions in the matter of religion which he reputed for damnable idolatry?[33] If man and angels would affirm that he will or may do it, his own verity shall convict them of a lie. For this sentence he pronounceth: "Not that which seemeth good in thy eyes shalt thou do to the Lord thy God, but that which the Lord thy God hath commanded thee, that do thou; add nothing unto it, diminish nothing from it."[34] Which, sealing up his New Testament, he repeateth in these words: "That which ye have, hold till I come," etc.[35] And therefore yet again it repenteth me not to say in this point, which is chief and principal, your Grace must disassent from the multitude of rulers, or else ye can possess no portion with Christ Jesus in his kingdom and glory.

Addition

Knowing by what craft Satan laboreth continually to keep the world in blindness, I added these two former points, to wit, that ye should not think yourself free from the reformation of religion because ye have bishops within your realm, neither yet that ye should judge that religion most perfect which the multitude by wrong custom hath embraced. In these two points doth Satan busily travail: first, that no civil magistrate presume to take cognition in the cause of religion, for that must be deferred to the determinations of the church; secondarily, that impossible it is that that religion should be false which so long time so many councils, and so great a multitude of men, so divers nations and realms have allowed, authorized, and confirmed. What is the duty of magistrates and what power the people hath in such cases granted by God, my purpose is to write in several letters to the nobility and estates of the realm, and therefore, to avoid tediousness and repetition of one thing, I now supersede. And as touching the second, if ye rightly consider the testimonies of Scriptures which I have before adduced, I trust ye shall find that objection sufficiently answered. For if the opinion of the multitude ought always to be preferred, then did God injury to the original world; for they were all of one mind, to wit, conjured against God, except Noah and his family.

And if antiquity of time shall be considered in such cases, then shall not only the idolatry of the gentiles but also the false religion of Mahomet be preferred to the papistry. For both the one and the other is more ancient than is the papistical religion; yea, Mahomet had established his Alcoran before any pope in Rome was crowned with a triple crown. But as touching antiquity, I am content with Tertullian to say, "let that be the most pure and perfect religion which shall be proved most ancient."[36] For this is a chief point wherein I will join with all the papists in the earth: that their religion, such as it is this day, is not of such antiquity as is that which we contend to be the true and only religion acceptable before God; neither yet that their church is the Catholic church, but that it is of late days in respect of Christ's institution, crept in and devised by man; and therefore am bold to affirm it odious and abominable.

For this is our chief proposition: that in the religion of God only ought his own word to be considered, that no authority of man nor angel ought in that case to be respected. And, as for their councils, when the matter shall come to trial, it shall be easily seen for whom the most godly and most ancient councils shall most plainly speak. I will prove by a council that of more authority is the sentence of one man, founded upon the simple truth of God, than is the determination of the whole council without the assurance of God's word.[37] But that all their determinations which we impugn are not only maintained without any assurance of Scriptures, but also are established against the truth of the same, yea, and for the most part against the decrees of the former councils, I offer myself evidently to prove. But now shortly to the rest of the former letter.

Letter

An orator and God's messenger also justly might require of you, now by God's hand promoted to high dignity, a motherly pity upon your subjects, a justice inflexible to be used against murderers and common oppressors, a heart void of avarice and partiality, a mind studious and careful for maintenance of that realm and commonwealth above whom God hath placed you, and by it hath made you honorable, with the rest of virtues which not only God's Scriptures but also writers illuminated only with the light of nature require in godly rulers. But vain it is to crave reformation of manners where religion is corrupted. For like as a man cannot do the office of a man till first he have a being and life, so to work works pleasant in the sight of God the father can no man do without the spirit of the Lord Jesus, which doth not abide in the hearts of idolaters. And therefore the most godly princes, Josiah, Hezekiah, and Jehoshaphat, seeking God's favor to rest upon them and upon their people, before all things, began to reform the religion.[38] For it is as the stomach within the body which, if it be corrupted, of necessity it infecteth the whole mass. And therefore (often I repeat that which to be done is most necessary), if your Grace pretend to reign with Christ Jesus, then it behooveth you to take care of his true religion which this day within your realm is so deformed that no part of Christ's ordinances remain in their first strength and original purity, which, I praise God, to me is less difficile to prove than dangerous to speak. And yet neither the one nor the other I fear; partly because the love of life eternal quencheth the terror of temporal death, and partly because I would with St. Paul wish myself accursed from Christ—as touching earthly pleasure—for the salvation of my brethren and illumination of your Grace, which thing, work, and very deed, and not bare word or writing shall witness and declare, if I may purchase the liberty of tongue but forty days only.

Addition

The wise and facund[39] Democritus had sometimes a familiar sentence: "That honest it was to commend such works as were worthy of praise, but to praise things that were wicked could not proceed but from a deceivable mind."[40] And Themistius, a philosopher of great fame, seeing the hall of Jovinian the Roman Emperor replenished with flatterers said, "of their manners it may be espied that more they worship the scepter and the purple than God," signifying that they little regarded whether the Emperor was godly or ungodly so that they might retain themselves in favor with him.[41] Albeit that those were ethnics and neither had knowledge of God, as we pretend, neither had given so plain a confession to declare themselves enemies to all iniquity, as we have done by baptism and by our whole profession of Christianity; yet do their words damn no small number of us, and chiefly such as be conversant with princes. For who in these miserable days judgeth himself to have offended, albeit he praise, allow, and maintain whatsoever the princes and upper powers devise? Yea, although it be to oppress and to spoil the poor, to pull from their skins, and as the Prophet saith, "to break their bones and to cut them in pieces, as flesh for the cauldron or pot," yet I say that the princes shall not lack judges to cry, "it is right, it is for the commonwealth, for defense of the realm, and ease of the subjects." So that the estate of times is even now such as when the Prophet complained, saying, "The princes ask, and the judge is ready to give, not his own, but the life and blood of the poor."[42]

How soon a great man hath spoken the corruption of his mind, he hath his flatterers ready to applaud and confirm whatsoever he speaketh. And let the princes be of what religion they please, that is all one to the most part of men, so that with abnegation of God, of his honor, and religion they may retain the friendship of the court. But, alas, how miserable be princes that so are abused, and how contagious a pestilence be such flatterers to commonwealths, empires, and realms, God hath declared even from the beginning to paint out the mischief which from them proceedeth to such as give ear unto them. The ancient writers compare them to harlots, to ravens, and to more ravenous beasts, and not without cause. For as harlots can never abide that their lovers should return to repentance and soberness of mind, so cannot flatterers sustain that such as they deceive shall come to right judgment. And as ravens pick out the eyes of dead carrions, and as ravenous beasts devour the same, so do flatterers, being more cruel, pick at the eyes of living men, and blinding the eyes of their understanding and judgment, do expone them to be devoured in body and soul to Satan.

This we have by profane writers only, but the Holy Spirit taught us this infallible truth: that where iniquity reigneth in a commonwealth, and none is found boldly and openly to reprehend the same, that there shall sudden vengeance and destruction follow. For thus it is written and pronounced by the Prophet Ezekiel: "Shalt thou not judge the city of blood which had made idols, whose rulers shed blood to the uttermost of their power? They have despised my holy things; they have devised iniquity and have performed the same. The conjuration of prophets hath gathered up the riches and whatsoever is precious within the same. The priests violently have torn and rent my law. The people of the land hath wrought deceitfully. They have oppressed the poor and have done violence to the stranger without judgment. And I have sought of them a man to repair the hedge and to stand in the gap before me, but I have found none. Therefore have I poured forth my wrath upon them, and in the fire of my hot displeasure I have consumed them."[43] Advert Madam, for these are not the words of mortal man but of the eternal God, and were not spoken against Jerusalem only but against every realm and nation that so offendeth. The sins that here be named are idolatry in all, avarice and cruelty in the princes and rulers, conjuration of the prophets to defend the wicked, deceit, fraud, and violence in the common people, and finally, an universal silence of all man, none being found to reprehend these enormities.

Would to God that I might with safety of conscience excuse you, your council, and the idolaters of that realm from any of these crimes aforenamed. The idolatry which is committed is more evident than that it can be denied; the avarice and cruelty, as well of your fellows as of such as be in authority, may be known by the facts. For fame carrieth the voices of the poor, oppressed by intolerable taxes, not only to us here in a strange country, but, I am assured, to the ears of the God of hosts. The conspiracy and conjuration of your false prophets is known to the world, and yet is none found so faithful to God nor merciful to your Grace that freely will and dare admonish you to repent before that God rise himself in judgment. When I name repentance, I mean no outward show of holiness, which commonly is found in hypocrites, but I mean a true conversion to the Lord God from your whole heart, with a damning of all superstition and idolatry, in which ye have been nourished, which with your presence yet have decored, and to your power maintained and defended. Unless, I say, that this poison be purged from your heart, be your outward life never so glittering before the world, yet in the presence of God it is but abominable. Yea, further I say, that where this venom of the serpent—idolatry, I mean—lurketh in the heart, it is impossible but that at one time or other it shall produce pestilent fruits, albeit, peradventure, not openly before men, yet before God no less odious than the facts of murderers, publicans, and harlots. And therefore in my former letter I said that superfluous it was to require reformation of manners where the religion is corrupted, which yet again I repeat to the end that your Grace more deeply may weigh the matter.⁴⁴ But now the rest of the same, my former letter.

Letter

I am not ignorant how dangerous a thing it appeareth to the natural man to innovate anything in matters of religion, and partly I consider that your Grace's power is not so free as a public reformation perchance would require. But if your Grace shall consider the danger and damnation perpetual which inevitably hangeth upon all maintainers of a false religion, then shall the greatest danger easily devour and swallow up the smaller. If your Grace shall consider that either ye must serve God to life everlasting or else serve the world to death and damnation, then albeit that man and angel should dissuade you, ye will choose life and refuse death.[45] And if further ye shall consider that the very life consisteth in the knowledge of the only true God and of his son Christ Jesus, and that true knowledge hath annexed with it God's true worship and honor which requireth a testimony of his own will expressed by his word that such honor doth please him, if these things aforesaid your Grace do earnestly meditate, then albeit ye may not do suddenly what ye would, yet shall ye not cease to do what ye may. Your Grace cannot hastily abolish superstition and remove from offices unprofitable pastors, of whom speaketh Ezekiel the Prophet, which to a public reformation is requisite and necessary.[46] But if the zeal of God's glory be fervent in your Grace's heart, ye will not by wicked laws maintain idolatry, neither will ye suffer the fury of bishops to murder and devour the poor members of Christ's body, as in times by past they have been accustomed; which thing, if either by blind ignorance ye do or yet for pleasure of others within this realm permit to be done, then, except you speedily repent, ye and your posterity shall suddenly feel the depressing hand of him who hath exalted you. Ye shall be compelled, will ye or not, to know that he is eternal against whom ye address the battle; and that it is he that moderateth the times and disposeth kingdoms, ejecting from authority such as be inobedient, and placing others according to his good pleasure; that it is he that glorifieth them that do glorify him and poureth forth contempt upon princes that rebel against his graces offered.[47]

Addition

In writing of this parcel, as I remembered the impediments which might call you back from God and from his true obedience, so did I consider what occasion ye had to tremble and to fear before his majesty and to enterprise the loss of all worldly glory for the promoting of the glory of God. I do consider that your power is but borrowed, extraordinary, and unstable, for ye have it but by permission of others. And seldom it is that women do long reign with felicity and joy. For as nature hath denied to them a constant spirit of good government, so hath God pronounced that they are never given to reign over men but in his wrath and indignation.[48] Your most especial friends moreover, blinded by the vanity of this world, yea, being drunken with the cup of that Roman harlot, are mortal enemies to Christ Jesus and to his true religion. These things may easily abash the mind of a woman; but yet if ye shall a little consider with me the causes why that ye ought to hazard all for the glory of God in this behalf, the former terrors shall suddenly vanish. I do not esteem that thing greatest which, peradventure, some others do, to wit, that if ye shall enterprise to innovate anything in matters of religion, that then ye shall lose your authority and also the favors of your carnal friends. I look further, to wit, to the judgments of God who hath begun already to declare himself angry with you, with your seed and posterity, yea, with the whole realm above which it should have ruled.

Impute not to fortune that first, your two sons were suddenly taken from you within the space of six hours, and after, your husand reft, as it were, by violence from life and honor, the memorial of his name, succession, and royal dignity perishing with himself.[49] For albeit the usurped abuse, or rather tyranny, of some realms have permitted women to succeed to the honor of their fathers, yet must their glory be transferred to the house of a stranger. And so I say that with himself was buried his name, succession, and royal dignity; and in this, if ye espy not the anger and hot displeasure of God, threatening you and the rest of your house with the same plague, ye are more obstinate than I would wish you to be. I would ye should ponder and consider deeply with yourself that God useth not to punish realms and nations with such rare plagues without great cause, neither useth he to restore to honors and glory the house which he beginneth once to deject, till repentance of the former crimes be found. Ye may, perchance, doubt what crimes should have been in your husband, you, or the realm for the which God should so grievously have punished you. I answer: the maintenance and defense of most horrible idolatry with the shedding of the blood of the saints of God who labored to notify and rebuke the same, this, I say—other iniquities omitted— is such a crime before the eyes of his majesty that for the same he hath poured forth his extreme vengeance upon kings and upon their posterity, depriving them from honors and dignity forever, as by the histories of the Books of the Kings is most evident.

To Jeroboam it is said: "Because I have exalted thee from the midst of the people and have made thee prince over my people Israel, I have rent the kingdom from the house of David for idolatry also and have given it unto thee; but thou hast not been as David my servant," etc. "But thou hast done wickedly above all that have gone before thee. For thou hast made to thee other gods and molten images to provoke me, and hast cast me behind thy back. Therefore I shall bring affliction upon the house of Jeroboam, and I shall destroy to Jeroboam all that pisseth against the wall" (signifying thereby the male children), "and shall cast forth the posterity of Jeroboam, as dung is cast forth till it be consumed."[50] This sentence was not only executed against this idolater but also against the rest of idolaters in that realm as they succeeded one after another. For to Baasha, whom God used as instrument to root out the seed of Jeroboam, it is said: "Because thou hast walked in the way of Jeroboam and hast caused my people Israel sin, that thou shouldst provoke me in their sins, therefore shall I cut down the posterity of Baasha and the posterity of his house, and shall make thy house as the house of Jeroboam. He that shall die to Baasha in the city, him shall dogs eat; and he that shall die in the field, him shall the fowls devour."[51] Of the same cup and for the same cause drank Ela and Ahab, yea, and the posterity of Jehu, following the footsteps of their forefathers.[52] By these examples you may evidently espy that idolatry is the cause why God destroyeth the posterity of princes, not only of those that first invent abominations but also of such as follow and defend the same.

Consider, Madam, that God hath begun very sharply with you, taking from you, as it were together, two children and a husband. He hath begun, I say, to declare himself angry; beware that ye provoke not the eyes of his majesty. It will not be the haughty looks of the proud, the strength of your friends, nor multitude of men that can justify your cause in his presence, if ye presume to rebel against him; and against him ye rebel if ye deny my most humble request which I make in his name, and it is this: with hazard of mine own life I offer to prove that religion which now ye maintain to be false, deceivable, and abomination before God, and that I shall do by most evident testimonies of his blessed, holy, and infallible word. If this, I say, ye deny, rebelling against God, the favor of your friends shall little avail you when he shall declare himself enemy to you and to your posterity, which, assure yourself, he shall shortly do, if ye begin to display the banner of your malice against him.

Let not the prosperity of others, be they princes, queens, kings, or emperors, bolden you to contemn God and his loving admonition. They shall drink the cup of his wrath, every one in their rank as he hath appointed them. No realm in these quarters, except it that next lieth to you, hath he so manifestly stricken with his terrible rod as he hath done you and your realm.[53] And therefore it becometh you first to stoop, except that ye will have the threatenings pronounced by Isaiah the Prophet ratified upon you, to wit, "that your sudden destruction be as the rotten wall, and your breaking as the breaking of a potsherd which is broken without pity, so that no portion of it can be found able either to carry fire or water."[54] Whereby the Prophet doth signify that the proud contemners of God and of his admonition shall so perish from all honors that they shall have nothing worthy of a memorial behind them in the earth.[55] Yea, if they do leave anything, as it shall be unprofitable, so shall it be in execration and hatred to the elect of God. And therefore thus proceedeth my former letter.[56]

Letter

How dangerous that ever it shall appear to the flesh to obey God and to make war against the devil—the prince of darkness, pride, and superstition—yet, if your Grace look to have yourself and seed to continue in honor worldly and everlasting, subject yourself betimes under the hand of him that is omnipotent. Embrace his will, despise not his Testament, refuse not his graces offered. When he calleth upon you, withdraw not your ear. Be not led away with the vain opinion that your church cannot err. Be ye most assuredly persuaded that so far as in life ye see them degenerate from Christ's true Apostles, so in religion are they further corrupted. Lay the Book of God before your eyes, and let it be judge to that which I say.[57] Which if ye with fear and reverence obey, as did Josiah the admonitions of the Prophetess,[58] then shall he, by whom kings do reign,[59] crown your battle with double benediction and reward you with wisdom, riches, glory, honor, and long life in this your regiment temporal and with life everlasting when the king of all kings—whose members now do cry for your help—the Lord Jesus shall appear to judgment accompanied with his angels, before whom ye shall make accompt of your present regiment, when the proud and disobedient shall cry, "Mountains fall upon us and hide us from the face of the Lord."[60] But then it shall be too late, because they contemned his voice when he lovingly called.

God, the father of our Lord Jesus Christ, by the power of his Holy Spirit move your heart so to consider and accept the things that be said that they be not a testimony of your just condemnation in that great day of the Lord Jesus, to whose omnipotent Spirit I unfeignedly commit your Grace.

Addition

When Jeremiah the Prophet at the commandment of God had written the sermons, threatenings, and plagues which he had spoken against Israel and Judah and had commanded them to be read by Baruch his scribe because himself was excommunicated and forbidden to enter into the temple, by the providence of God it came to pass that Micaiah, the son of Gemariah, hearing the said sermons, passed to the King's house and did communicate the matter with the rest of the princes, who, also after they had read the same volume of Jeremiah's preachings, did not conceal the truth from King Jehoiakim, who then did reign in Jerusalem. But the proud and desperate prince, commanding the book to be read in his presence, before he had heard three of four leaves of the same, did cut it and cast it into the fire, notwithstanding that some of the princes—I think not all—made request in the contrary. But the Prophet was charged by God to write again and to say to Jehoiakim the King: "Thus saith the Lord: thou hast burnt this book, saying, why hast thou written in it according to this sentence? Assuredly the King of Babylon shall come and shall destroy this land and shall make it void of men and beasts. Therefore thus saith the Lord of Jehoiakim the King: there shall not be one left alive to sit in the seat of David. Their carcasses shall be cast to the heat of the day and to the frost of the night" (whereby the Prophet did signify the most vile contempt and most cruel torment), "and I shall visit the iniquity of himself, of his seed, and servants, and I shall bring upon them, and upon the inhabiters of Jerusalem, and upon all Judah all the calamities which I have spoken against them. Albeit they would not hear."[61]

This is not written, Madam, for that time only, but to assure us that the like punishment abideth the like contemners of what estate, condition or degree that ever they be. I did write unto you before, having testimony of a good conscience, that I did it in the fear of my God and by the motion of his Holy Spirit (for the request of faithful brethren in things lawful and appertaining to God's glory, I cannot but judge to be the voice of the Holy Ghost); but how ye did accept the same, my former writing, I do not otherwise than by conjectures understand. Whether ye did read it to the end or not, I am uncertain. One thing I know, that ye did deliver it to one of your prelates, saying, "my lord, will ye read a pasquil?"[62] As charity persuadeth me to interpret things doubtfully spoken in the best sense, so my duty to God, who hath commanded me to flatter no prince in the earth, compelleth me to say that if no more ye esteem the admonition of God nor the cardinals do the scoffing of pasquils, that then he shall shortly send you messengers with whom ye shall not be able on that manner to jest. If my person be considered, I grant my threatenings are no more to be feared than be the merry sports which fearful men do father upon Pasquillus in Rome. But Madam, if ye shall deeply consider that God useth men—yea, and most commonly those that be of lowest degree and most abject before the world—to be his messengers and ambassadors, not only to notify his will to the simple people, but also to rebuke the most proud tyrants and potent princes, then will ye not judge the liquor by the outward appearance and nature of the vessel. For ye are not ignorant that the most noble wine is inclosed within the tun made of frail wood, and that the precious ointment is often kept within the pot made of clay.[63] If further ye shall consider that God will do nothing touching the punishment of realms and nations which he will not reveal to his servants, the prophets, whose tongues he will compel to speak sometimes contrary to the appetites and desires of their own hearts, and whose words he will perform, be they never so unapparent to the judgment of men.[64]

If these ye do deeply weigh, then will ye fear the thing which presently is not seen. Elijah was but a man, as St. James doth witness, like to his brethren, and yet at his prayer was Ahab the idolater and all Israel with him punished three years and six months, God shutting up the heaven that neither rain nor dew fell upon the earth the space aforewritten.[65] And in the end God so wrought by him that Baal's priests were first confounded and after justly punished. And albeit that Jezebel sought his blood and by oath had determined his death, yet as she was frustrate of her intent, so could she not keep her own bones from the dogs, which punishment the Prophet—God so ruling his tongue—had before appointed to that wicked woman.[66]

Albeit, Madam, that the messengers of God are not sent this day with visible miracles, because they teach none other doctrine than that which is confirmed with miracles from the beginning of the world; yet will not he, who hath promised to take charge over his poor and little flock to the end, suffer the contempt of their embassade escape punishment and vengeance. For the truth itself hath said, "He that heareth you, heareth me, and he that contemneth you, contemneth me."[67] I did not speak unto you, Madam, by former letter, neither yet do I now, as Pasquillus doth to the pope and his carnal cardinals in the behalf of such as dare not utter their names; but I come in the name of Christ Jesus, affirming that the religion which ye maintain is damnable idolatry, the which I offer myself to prove by the most evident testimonies of God's Scriptures. And in this quarrel I present myself against all the papists within the realm, desiring none other armor but God's holy word and the liberty of my tongue. God move your heart to understand my petition, to know the truth, and unfeignedly to follow the same.

Amen

"I am the beginning and the end. I will give to him that is athirst of the well of the water of life freely. He that overcometh shall inherit all things, and I will be his God, and he shall be my son. But the fearful, and unbelieving, and the abominable, and murderers, and whoremongers, and sorcerers, and idolaters, and all liars shall have their part in the lake which burneth with fire and brimstone, which is the second death."[68]

Notes

1. [Knox was in Geneva when the ecclesiastical authorities in Scotland condemned him and burned his effigy.]
2. Gen. 3 : Matt. 10; Acts 14.
3. Matt. 5; John 14, 16.
4. Isa. 9.
5. Isa. 40, 41, 51; Exod. 2; 2 Kings 25; Ezra 1.
6. Eph. 2.
7. I John 1, 2; Heb. 6, 10; Eph. 5.
8. Matt. 23 : 35, 36.
9. Gen. 4.
10. Matt. 23.
11. Matt. 15 : 14.
12. Gen. 19; Exod. 14; Flavius Josephus *Antiquities of the Jews* xx.8.5.
13. Matt. 5, 10; 1 Cor. 2.
14. Matt. 10.
15. [The reference was to his important missionary work in 1556.]
16. Exod. 20; Rom. 13; 1 Pet. 2.
17. John 4; Rev. 14, 17.
18. Dan. 3, 6.
19. [Isa. 8 : 12.]
20. Matt. 10.
21. Acts 14.
22. Gen. 6.
23. Ps. 14.
24. Ps. 2; Acts 4.
25. Luke 18 : 8.
26. Hos. 4 : 1, 2.
27. Matt. 20 : 16.
28. Matt. 7.
29. 2 Thess. 2.
30. Deut. 14, 12.
31. Matt. 15 : 13.
32. 1 Kings 13, 15; 2 Chron. 26; Lev. 10.

33. Matt. 17; Acts 1, 2, 3; 1 Cor. 11; Col. 2.

34. Deut. 4:2; Deut. 12.

35. Rev. 2:25.

36. Tertullian, *Apology,* 14.19.2.

37. First Nicene Council

38. 1 Kings 15; 2 Chron. 17; 2 Kings 22, 23; 2 Chron. 34; 2 Kings 18; 2 Chron. 29, 30, 31.

39. [eloquent]

40. Fragment 63.

41. Nicepho Calistus *Hist. Eccl.* 10.42.

42. Mic. 3.

43. Ezek. 22.

44. Idolatry is mother to all vice.

45. Matt. 6; Rom. 8; 1 Kings 18; John 17.

46. Ezek. 34.

47. Dan. 2; 2 Kings 2; Job 12; Ps. 107.

48. Isa. 3.

49. [Her infant sons, James and Arthur, died in 1541; her husband, James V, died in December 1542.]

50. 1 Kings 14:10.

51. 1 Kings 16:2, 3.

52. 1 Kings 16; 2 Kings 10, 17.

53. No realm, England excepted, so grievously plagued as Scotland.

54. Isa. 30:14.

55. Isa. 14.

56. Ibid.

57. Josh. 1.

58. 2 Chron. 34.

59. 2 Chron. 1.

60. Rev. 6:16.

61. Jer. 36:29, 30, 31.

62. [The remark was made to James Beaton, Bishop of Glasgow, nephew to the murdered cardinal. The reference was to a Roman statue of Pasquino upon which defamatory verses were attached.]

63. Amos 3; Eccles. 4–7.

64. Zech. 1.

65. Jas. 5; 1 Kings 17, 18.

66. 1 Kings 19; 2 Kings 9.

67. Luke 10:16.

68. Rev. 21:6, 7, 8.

3

Appellation to the Nobility (1558)

The Appellation of John Knox from the cruel and most injust sentence pronounced against him by the false bishops of Scotland with his supplication and exhortation to the nobility, estates, and commonalty of the same realm.

To the nobility and estates of Scotland John Knox wisheth grace, mercy, and peace from God, the father of our lord Jesus Christ, with the spirit of righteous judgment.

It is not only the love of life temporal, right honorable, neither yet the fear of corporal death that moveth me at this present to expone[1] unto you the injuries done against me and to crave of you, as of lawful powers by God appointed, redress of the same; but partly it proceedeth from that reverence which every man oweth to God's eternal truth and partly from a love which I bear to your salvation and to the salvation of my brethren abused in that realm by such as have no fear of God before their eyes.

It hath pleased God of his infinite mercy not only so to illuminate the eyes of my mind and so to touch my dull heart that clearly I see and by his grace unfeignedly believe that, "there is no other name given to men under the heaven, in which salvation consisteth, save the name of Jesus alone,"[2] "Who by that sacrifice which he did once offer upon the cross hath sanctified forever those that shall inherit the kingdom promised."[3] But also it hath pleased him of his super-abundant grace to make and appoint me, most wretched of many thousands, a witness, minister, and preacher of the same doctrine. The sum whereof I did not spare to communicate with my brethren, being with them in the realm of Scotland in the year 1556, because I know myself to be a steward, and that accompts of the talent committed to my charge shall be required to him who will admit no vain excuse which fearful men pretend.[4] I did therefore, as God did minister, during the time I was conversant with them (God is record and witness), truly and sincerely, according to the gift granted unto me, divide the word of salvation, teaching all men to hate sin—which before God was and is so odious that none other sacrifice could satisfy his justice except the death of his only son; and to magnify the great mercies of our heavenly Father—who did not spare the substance of his glory but did give him to the world to suffer the ignominious and cruel death of the cross, by that means to reconcile his chosen children to himself; teaching further what is the duty of such as to believe themselves purged by such a price from their former filthiness, to wit, that they are bound to walk in the newness of life, fighting against the lusts of the flesh, and studying at all times to glorify God by such good works as he hath prepared his children to walk in.[5] In doctrine I did further affirm, so taught by my master Christ Jesus, that, "whosoever denieth him, yea, or is ashamed of him before this wicked generation, him shall Christ Jesus deny, and of him shall he be ashamed when he shall appear in majesty."[6] And therefore I fear not to affirm that of necessity it is that such as hope for life everlasting avoid all superstition, vain religion, and idolatry. Vain religion and idolatry I call whatsoever is done in God's service or honor without the express commandment of his own word.

This doctrine did I believe to be so conformable to God's Holy Scriptures that I thought no creature could have been so impudent as to have damned any point or article of the same. Yet nevertheless, me, as an heretic, and this doctrine as heretical have your false bishops and ungodly clergy damned, pronouncing against me a sentence of death, in testification whereof they have burned a picture.[7] From which false and cruel sentence and from all judgment of that wicked generation, I make it known to your honors that I appeal to a lawful and general council, to such, I mean, as the most ancient laws and canons do approve to be holden, by such as whose manifest impiety is not to be reformed in the same. Most humbly requiring of your honors that, as God hath appointed you princes in that people and by reason thereof requireth of your hands the defense of innocents troubled in your dominion, in the meantime, and till the controversies that this day be in religion be lawfully decided, ye receive me and such others, as most unjustly by those cruel beasts are persecuted, in your defense and protection.

Your honors are not ignorant that it is not I alone who doth sustain this cause against the pestilent generation of papists, but that the most part of Germany, the country of Helvetia, the King of Denmark, the nobility of Polonia, together with many other cities and churches reformed, appeal from the tyranny of that Antichrist and most earnestly do call for a lawful and general council wherein may all controversies in religion be decided by the authority of God's most sacred word. And unto this same, as said is, do I appeal yet once again, requiring of your honors to hold my simple and plain appellation of no less value nor effect than if it had been made with greater circumstance, solemnity, and ceremony, and that ye receive me, calling unto you as to the powers of God ordained, in your protection and defense against the rage of tyrants, not to maintain me in any iniquity, error, or false opinion but to let me have such equity as God by his word, ancient laws, and determinations of most godly councils grant to men accused or infamed.

The word of God will that no man shall die except he be found criminal and worthy of death for offence committed, of the which he must be manifestly convicted by two or three witnesses.[8] Ancient laws do permit just defenses to such as be accused (be their crimes never so horrible), and godly councils will that neither bishop nor person ecclesiastical whatsoever, accused of any crime, shall sit in judgment, consultation, or council where the cause of such men as do accuse them is to be tried. These things require I of your honors to be granted unto me, to wit, that the doctrine which our adversaries condemn for heresy may be tried by the simple and plain word of God, that just defenses be admitted to us that sustain the battle against this pestilent generation of Antichrist, and that they be removed from judgment in our cause, seeing that our accusation is not intended against any one particular person but against that whole kingdom which we doubt not to prove to be a power usurped against God, against his commandment, and against the ordinance of Christ Jesus established in his Church by his chief Apostles. Yea, we doubt not to prove the kingdom of the pope to be the kingdom and power of Antichrist. And therefore, my lords, I cannot cease in the name of Christ Jesus to require of you that the matter may come in examination, and that ye, the estates of the realm, by your authority compel such as will be called bishops not only to desist from their cruel murdering of such as do study to promote God's glory in detecting and disclosing the damnable impiety of that man of sin, the Roman Antichrist, but also that ye compel them to answer to such crimes as shall be laid to their charge for not righteously instructing the flock committed to their cares.

But here I know two things shall be doubted. The former, whether that my appellation is lawful and to be admitted, seeing that I am damned as an heretic; and secondarily, whether your honors be bound to defend such as call for your support in that case, seeing that your bishops, who in matters of religion claim all authority to appertain to them, have by their sentence already condemned me. The one and the other I nothing doubt most clearly to prove: first, that my appellation is most lawful and just; and secondarily, that your honors cannot refuse to defend me, thus calling for your aid, but that in so doing ye declare yourselves rebellious to God, maintainers of murderers, and shedders of innocent blood.

How just cause I have by the civil law (as for their canon, it is accursed of God) to appeal from their unjust sentence, my purpose is not to make long discourse. Only I will touch the points which all men confess to be just causes of appellation. First, lawfully could I not be summoned by them, being for that time absent from their jurisdiction, charged with the preaching of Christ's Evangel in a free city not subject to their tyranny. Secondarily, to me was no intimation made of their summons, but so secret was their surmised malice that, the copy of the summons being required, was denied. Thirdly, to the realm of Scotland could I have had no free nor sure access, being before exiled from the same by their unjust tyranny. And last, to me they neither could nor can be competent and indifferent judges; for that before any summons were raised against me, I had accused them by my letters published to the Queen Dowager and had intended against them all crimes, offering myself with hazard of life to prove the same, for the which they are not only unworthy of ecclesiastical authority but also of any sufferance within a commonwealth professing Christ.

This, my accusation, preceding their summons, neither by the law of God neither yet by the law of man can they be to me competent judges till place be granted unto me openly to prove my accusation intended against them and they be compelled to make answer as criminals. For I will plainly prove that not only bishops but also popes have been removed from all authority and pronouncing of judgment till they have purged themselves of accusations laid against them. Yea, further I will prove that bishops and popes most justly have been deprived from all honors and administration for smaller crimes than I have to charge the whole rabble of your bishops. But because this is not my chief ground, I will stand content for this present to shew that lawful it is to God's prophets and to preachers of Christ Jesus to appeal from the sentence and judgment of the visible church to the knowledge of the temporal magistrate, who by God's law is bound to hear their causes and to defend them from tyranny.

The Prophet Jeremiah was commanded by God to stand in the court of the house of the Lord and to preach this sermon in effect: that Jerusalem should be destroyed and be exponed in opprobry, to all nations of the earth, and that also that famous temple of God should be made desolate, like unto Shiloh, because the priests, the prophets, and the people did not walk in the law which God had proposed unto them, neither would they obey the voices of the prophets whom God sent to call them to repentance.[9] For this sermon was Jeremiah apprehended, and a sentence of death was pronounced against him and that by the priests, by the prophets, and by the people; which things being bruited in the ears of the princes of Judah, they passed up from the king's house to the temple of the Lord and sat down in judgment for further knowledge of the cause. But the priests and prophets continued in their cruel sentence, which before they had pronounced, saying, "This man is worthy of the death, for he hath prophesied against this city as your ears have heard." But Jeremiah, so moved by the Holy Ghost, began his defense against that their tyrannous sentence in these words: "The Lord," saith he, "hath sent me to prophesy against this house and against this city all the words which you have heard. Now therefore make good your ways and hear the voice of the Lord your God, and then shall he repent of the evil which he hath spoken against you. As for me, behold I am in your hands" (so doth he speak to the princes), "do to me as you think good and righteous. Nevertheless know you this most assuredly, that if ye murder or slay me, ye shall make yourselves, this city, and the inhabitants of the same criminal and guilty of innocent blood. For of a truth the Lord hath sent me to speak in your ears all those words." Then the princes and the people, saith the text, said, "this man is not worthy of death, for he hath spoken to us in the name of the Lord our God." And so after some contention was the Prophet delivered from that danger.

This fact and history manifestly proveth whatsoever before I have affirmed, to wit, that it is lawful for the servants of God to call for the help of the civil magistrate against the sentence of death if it be unjust, by whomsoever it be pronounced, and also that the civil sword hath power to repress the fury of the priests and to absolve whom they have condemned. For the Prophet of God was damned by those who then only in earth were known to be the visible church, to wit, priests and prophets who then were in Jerusalem, the successors of Aaron to whom was given a charge to speak to the people in the name of God, and a precept given to the people to hear the law from their mouths—to the which if any should be rebellious or inobedient, he should die the death without mercy.[10] These men, I say, thus authorized by God first did excommunicate Jeremiah for that he did preach otherwise than did the common sort of prophets in Jerusalem, and last apprehended him, as you have heard, pronouncing against him this sentence aforewritten, from the which, nevertheless, the Prophet appealed—that is, sought help and defense against the same, and that most earnestly did he crave of the princes. For albeit he saith, "I am in your hands, do with me as ye think righteous," he doth not contemn nor neglect his life as though he regarded not what should become of him, but in those his words most vehemently did he admonish the princes and rulers of the people, giving them to understand what God should require of them.[11]

As he should say: "You princes of Judah and rulers of the people, to whom appertaineth indifferently to judge betwixt party and party, to justify the just man, and to condemn the malefactor, you have heard a sentence of death pronounced against me by those whose lips ought to speak no decept because they are sanctified and appointed by God himself to speak his law and pronounce judgment with equity; but as they have left the living God and have taught the people to follow vanity, so are they becomed mortal enemies to all God's true servants, of whom I am one, rebuking their iniquity, apostasy, and defection from God which is the only cause they seek my life. But a thing most contrary to all equity, law, and justice it is that I, a man sent of God to call them, this people, and you again to the true service of God, from the which you are all declined, shall suffer the death because that my enemies do so pronounce sentence. I stand in your presence, whom God hath made princes; your power is above their tyranny; before you do I expone my cause. I am in your hands and cannot resist to suffer what ye think just. But lest that my lenity and patience should either make you negligent in the defense of me in my just cause appealing to your judgment, either yet encourage my enemies in seeking my blood, this one thing I dare not conceal: that if you murder me (which thing ye do if ye defend me not), ye make not only my enemies guilty of my blood but also yourselves and this whole city."

By these words, I say, it is evident that the Prophet of God, being damned to death by the priests and the prophets of the visible church, did seek aid, support, and defense at the princes and temporal magistrates, threatening his blood to be required of their hands if they by their authority did not defend him from the fury of his enemies, alleging also just cause of his appellation and why he ought to have been defended, to wit, that he was sent of God to rebuke their vices and defection from God, that he taught no doctrine which God before had not pronounced in his law, that he desired their conversion to God, continually calling upon them to walk in ways which God had approved, and therefore doth he boldly crave of the princes, as of God's lieutenants, to be defended from the blind rage and tyranny of the priests, notwithstanding that they claimed to themselves authority to judge in all matters of religion.

And the same did he what time he was cast in prison and thereafter was brought to the presence of King Zedekiah. After, I say, that he had defended his innocence, affirming that he neither had offended against the King, against his servants, nor against the people, at last he made intercession to the King for his life, saying, "But now my Lord the King take heed, I beseech thee, let my prayer fall into thy presence, command me not to be carried again into the house of Jonathan the scribe that I die not there." And the text witnesseth that the King commanded the place of his imprisonment to be changed.[12] Whereof it is evident that the Prophet did ofter than once seek help at the civil power, and that first the princes and thereafter the King did acknowledge that it appertained to their office to deliver him from the injust sentence which was pronounced against him.

If any think that Jeremiah did not appeal because he only declared the wrong done unto him and did but crave defense according to his innocence, let the same man understand that none otherwise do I appeal from that false and cruel sentence which your bishops have pronounced against me. Neither yet can there be any other just cause of appellation but innocence hurt or suspected to be hurt, whether it be by ignorance of a judge or by malice and corruption of those who under the title of justice do exercise tyranny. If I were a thief, murderer, blasphemer, open adulterer, or any offender whom God's word commandeth to suffer for a crime committed, my appellation were vain and to be rejected; but I being innocent (yea, the doctrine which your bishops have condemned in me being God's eternal verity), have no less liberty to crave your defense against that cruelty than had the Prophet Jeremiah to seek the aid of the princes and King of Judah.

But this shall more plainly appear in the fact[13] of St. Paul, who, after that he was apprehended in Jerusalem, did first claim to the liberty of Roman citizens for avoiding torment what time that the captain would have examined him by questions. Thereafter in the council, where no righteous judgment was to be hoped for, he affirmed that he was a Pharisee and that he was accused of the resurrection of the dead. And last in the presence of Festus he appealed from all knowledge and judgment in the priests of Jerusalem to the Emperor (of which last point, because it doth chiefly appertain to this my cause, I will somewhat speak).[14]

After that Paul had divers times been accused, as in the Acts of the Apostles it is manifest, at the last the chief priests and their faction came to Caesarea with Festus the president, who presented to them Paul in judgment, whom they accused of horrible crimes, which nevertheless they could not prove, the Apostle defending that he had not offended neither against the law, neither against the temple, neither yet against the Emperor. But Festus, willing to gratify the Jews, said to Paul, "Wilt thou go up to Jerusalem, and there be judged of these things in my presence?" But Paul said, "I stand at the justice seat of the Emperor where it behooveth me to be judged. I have done no injury to the Jews, as thou better knowest. If I have done anything injustly, or yet committed crime worthy of death, I refuse not to die; but if there be nothing of these things true whereof they accuse me, no man may give me to them. I appeal to Caesar."[15]

It may appear at the first sight that Paul did great injury to Festus, the judge, and to the whole order of the priesthood, who did hope greater equity in a cruel tyrant than in all that session and learned company. Which thing no doubt Festus did understand, pronouncing these words: "Hast thou appealed to Caesar? Thou shalt go to Caesar." As he would say: "I, as a man willing to understand the truth before I pronounce sentence, have required of thee to go to Jerusalem where the learned of thine own nation may hear thy cause and discern in the same. The controversy standeth in matters of religion. Thou art accused as an apostate from the law, as a violator of the temple, and transgressor of the traditions of their fathers, in which matters I am ignorant and therefore desire information by those that be learned in the same religion whereof the question is. And yet dost thou refuse so many godly fathers to hear thy cause and dost appeal to the Emperor, preferring him to all our judgments, of no purpose belike but to delay time."

Thus, I say, it might have appeared that Paul did not only injury to the judge and to the priests, but also that his cause was greatly to be suspected—partly for that he did refuse the judgment of those that had most knowledge, as all men supposed, of God's will and religion, and partly because he appealed to the Emperor, who then was at Rome far absent from Jerusalem, a man also ignorant of God and enemy to all virtue. But the Apostle, considering the nature of his enemies and what things they had intended against him even from the first day that he began freely to speak in the name of Christ, did not fear to appeal from them and from the judge that would have gratified them. They had professed themselves plain enemies of Christ Jesus and to his blessed Evangel, and had sought the death of Paul, yea, even by factions and treasonable conspiracy, and therefore by no means would he admit them either judges in his cause, either auditors of the same as Festus required. But grounding himself upon strong reasons, to wit, that he had not offended the Jews, neither yet the law, but that he was innocent, and therefore that no judge ought to give him in the hands of his enemies; grounding, I say, his appellation upon these reasons, he neither regarded the displeasure of Festus, neither yet the bruit of the ignorant multitude, but boldly did appeal from all cognition of them to the judgment of the Emperor, as said is.

By these two examples I doubt not but your honors do understand that lawful it is to the servants of God, oppressed by tyranny, to seek remedy against the same, be it by appellation from their sentence or by imploring the help of civil magistrates. For what God hath approved in Jeremiah and Paul, he can condemn in none that likewise be entreated. I might allege some histories of the primitive church serving to the same purpose: as of Ambrose and Athanasius, of whom the one would not be judged but at Milan where that his doctrine was heard of all his church and received and approved by many; and the other would in nowise give place to those councils where he knew that men, conspired against the truth of God, should sit in judgment and consultation. But because the Scriptures of God are my only foundation and assurance in all matters of weight and importance, I have thought the two former testimonies sufficient as well to prove my appellation reasonable and just, as to declare to your honors that with safe conscience ye cannot refuse to admit the same.

If any think it arrogance or foolishness in me to compare myself with Jeremiah and Paul, let the same man understand that, as God is immutable, so is the verity of his glorious Evangel of equal dignity whensoever it is impugned, be the members suffering never so weak. What I think touching mine own person God shall reveal when the secrets of all hearts shall be disclosed, and such as with whom I have been conversant can partly witness what arrogance or pride they espy in me. But touching the doctrine and cause which that adulterous and pestilent generation of Antichrist's servants— who will be called bishops amongst you—have condemned in me, I neither fear nor shame to confess and avow before man and angel to be the eternal truth of the eternal God. And in that case I doubt not to compare myself with any member in whom the truth hath been impugned since the beginning, for as it was the truth which Jeremiah did preach in these words: "The priests have not known me, saith the Lord, but the pastors have traitorously declined and fallen back from me. The prophets have prophesied in Baal and have gone after those things which cannot help. My people have left the fountain of living waters and have digged to themselves pits which can contain no water."[16]

As it was a truth that the pastors and watchmen in the days of Isaiah were becomed dumb dogs, blind, ignorant, proud, and avaricious, and finally as it was a truth that the princes and the priests were murderers of Christ Jesus and cruel persecutors of his Apostles, so likewise it is a truth—and that most infallible—that those that have condemned me (the whole rabble of the papistical clergy) have declined from the true faith, have given ear to deceivable spirits and to doctrine of devils, are the stars fallen from the heaven to the earth, are fountains without water, and finally are enemies to Christ Jesus, deniers of his virtue, and horrible blasphemers of his death and passion.[17] And further, as that visible church had no crime whereof justly they could accuse either the Prophets either the Apostles, except their doctrine, so have not such as seek my blood other crime to lay to my charge except that I affirm, as always I offer to prove, that the religion which now is maintained by fire and sword is no less contrarious to the true religion taught and established by the Apostles than is darkness to light, or the devil to God, and also that such as now do claim the title and name of the church are no more the elect spouse of Christ Jesus than was the synagogue of the Jews the true church of God what time it crucified Christ Jesus, damned his doctrine, and persecuted his Apostles. And therefore, seeing that my battle is against the proud and cruel hypocrites of this age as that battle of those most excellent instruments was against the false prophets and malignant church of their ages, neither ought any man think it strange that I compare myself with them with whom I sustain a common cause, neither ought you, my lords, judge yourselves less addebted and bound to me, calling for your support, than did the princes of Judah think themselves bound to Jeremiah, whom for that time they delivered notwithstanding the sentence of death pronounced against him by the visible church. And thus much for the right of my appellation which in the bowels of Christ Jesus I require your honors not to esteem as a thing superfluous and vain but that ye admit and also accept me in your protection and defense that, by you assured, I may have access to my native country, which I never offended, to the end that freely and openly in the presence of the whole realm I may give my confession of all such points as this day be in controversy, and also that you, by your authority which ye have of God, compel such as of long time have blinded and deceived both yourselves and the people to answer to such things as shall be laid to their charge.

But, lest some doubt remain that I require more of you than you of conscience are bound to grant, in few words I hope to prove my petition to be such, as without God's heavy displeasure, ye cannot deny. My petition is that ye, whom God hath appointed heads in your commonwealth, with single eye do study to promote the glory of God, to provide that your subjects be rightly instructed in his true religion, that they be defended from all oppression and tyranny, that true teachers may be maintained, and such as blind and deceive the people together also with all idle bellies which do rob and oppress the flock may be removed and punished as God's law prescribeth. And to the performance of every one of these do your offices and names, the honors and benefits which ye receive, the law of God universally given to all men, and the examples of most goldly princes, bind and oblige you.

My purpose is not greatly to labor to prove that your whole study ought to be to promote the glory of God; neither yet will I study to allege all reasons that justly may be brought to prove that ye are not exalted to reign above your brethren as men without care and solicitude. For these be principles so grafted in nature that very ethnics have confessed the same. For seeing that God only hath placed you in his chair, hath appointed you to be his lieutenants, and by his own seal hath marked you to be magistrates and to rule above your brethren, to whom nature nevertheless hath made you like in all points (for in conception, birth, life, and death ye differ nothing from the common sort of men, but God only, as said is, hath promoted you and of his especial favor hath given unto you this prerogative to be called gods), how horrible ingratitude were it then that you should be found unfaithful to him that thus hath honored you. And further what a monster were it that you should be proved unmerciful to them above whom ye are appointed to reign as fathers above their children. Because I say that very ethnics have granted that the chief and first care of princes and of such as be appointed to rule above others ought to be to promote the glory and honor of their gods and to maintain that religion which they supposed to have been true, and that their second care was to maintain and defend the subjects committed to their charge in all equity and justice, I will not labor to shew unto you what ought to be your study in maintaining God's true honor, lest that in so doing I should seem to make you less careful over God's true religion than were the ethnics over their idolatry.

But because other petitions may appear more hard and difficile to be granted, I purpose briefly but yet freely to speak what God by his word doth assure me to be true: to wit, first, that in conscience you are bound to punish malefactors and to defend innocents imploring your help; secondarily, that God requireth of you to provide that your subjects be rightly instructed in his true religion and that the same by you be reformed whensoever abuses do creep in by malice of Satan and negligence of men; and last, that ye are bound to remove from honor and to punish with death—if the crime so require—such as deceive the people or defraud them of that food of their souls—I mean God's lively word.

The first and second are most plain by the words of St. Paul, thus speaking of lawful powers: "Let every soul," saith he, "submit himself unto the higher powers. For there is no power but of God. The powers that be are ordained of God, and they that resist shall receive to themselves damnation. For rulers are not to be feared of those that do well, but of those that do evil. Wilt thou then be without fear of the power? Do that which is good, and so shalt thou be praised of the same. For he is the minister of God for thy wealth. But if thou do that which is evil, fear. For he beareth not the sword for nought, for he is the minister of God to take vengeance on them that do evil."[18]

As the Apostle in these words most straitly commandeth obedience to be given to lawful powers, pronouncing God's wrath and vengeance against such as shall resist the ordinance of God, so doth he assign to the powers their offices which be to take vengeance upon evil-doers, to maintain the well-doers, and so to minister and rule in their office that the subjects by them may have a benefit and be praised in well doing. Now if you be powers ordained by God—and that I hope all men will grant, then by the plain words of the Apostle is the sword given unto you by God for maintenance of the innocent and for punishment of malefactors. But I and my brethren with me accused do offer not only to prove ourselves innocents in all things laid to our charge but also we offer most evidently to prove your bishops to be the very pestilence who have infected all Christianity. And therefore by the plain doctrine of the Apostle you are bound to maintain us and to punish the other, being convict and proved criminal.

Moreover the former words of the Apostle do teach how far high powers be bound to their subjects, to wit, that because they are God's ministers by him ordained for the profit and utility of others, most diligently ought they to intend upon the same. For that cause assigneth the Holy Ghost, commanding subjects to obey and to pay tribute, saying, "for this do you pay tribute and toll," that is, because they are God's ministers, bearing the sword for your utility.[19] Whereof it is plain that there is no honor without a charge annexed. And this one point I wish your wisdoms deeply to consider: that God hath not placed you above your brethren to reign as tyrants without respect of their profit and commodity. You hear the Holy Ghost witness the contrary, affirming that all lawful powers be God's ministers ordained for the wealth, profit, and salvation of their subjects and not for their destruction. Could it be said, I beseech you, that magistrates, enclosing their subjects in a city without all victuals or giving unto them no other victuals but such as were poisoned, did rule for the profit of their subjects? I trust that none would be so foolish as so to affirm, but that rather every discreet person would boldly affirm that such as so did were tyrants unworthy of all regiment. If we will not deny that which Christ Jesus affirmeth to be a truth infallible, to wit, that the soul is greater and more precious than is the body, then shall we easily espy how unworthy of authority be those that this day debar their subjects from the hearing of God's word and by fire and sword compel them to feed upon the very poison of their souls—the damnable doctrine of Antichrist. And therefore in this point I say I cannot cease to admonish your honors diligently to take heed over your charge, which is greater than the most part of men suppose.

It is not enough that you abstain from violent wrong and oppression, which ungodly men exercise against their subjects; but ye are further bound, to wit, that ye rule above them for their wealth, which ye cannot do if that ye either by negligence, not providing true pastors, or yet by your maintenance of such as be ravening wolves suffer their souls to starve and perish for lack of the true food which is Christ's Evangel sincerely preached. It will not excuse you in his presence, who will require accompt of every talent committed to your charge, to say that ye supposed that the charge of the souls had been committed to your bishops. No, no, my lords, for ye cannot escape God's judgment. For if your bishops be proved to be no bishops but deceivable thieves and ravening wolves (which I offer myself to prove by God's word, by law and councils, yea, by the judgment of all the godly learned from the primitive church to this day), then shall your permission and defense of them be reputed before God a participation with their theft and murder. For thus accused the Prophet Isaiah the princes of Jerusalem: "Thy princes," saith he, "are apostates," that is, obstinate refusers of God, "and they are companions of thieves."[20] This grievous accusation was laid against them (albeit that they ruled in that city which sometime was called holy, where then were the temple, rites, and ordinances of God), because that not only they were wicked themselves but chiefly because they maintained wicked men, their priests and false prophets, in honors and authority. If they did not escape this accusation of the Holy Ghost in that age, look ye neither to escape the accusation nor judgment which is pronounced against the maintainers of wicked men, to wit, that the one and the other shall drink the cup of God's wrath and vengeance together.[21]

And, lest ye should deceive yourselves, esteeming your bishops to be virtuous and godly, this do I affirm and offer myself to prove the same: that more wicked men than be the whole rabble of your clergy were never from the beginning universally known in any age; yea, Sodom and Gomorrah may be justified in their respect. For they permitted just Lot to dwell amongst them without any violence done to his body, which that pestilent generation of your shaven sort doth not but most cruelly persecute by fire and sword the true members of Christ's body for no other cause but for the true service and honoring of God.

And therefore I fear not to affirm that which God shall one day justify: that by your offices ye be bound not only to repress their tyranny but also to punish them as thieves and murderers, as idolaters and blasphemers of God; and in their rooms ye are bound to place true preachers of Christ's Evangel for the instruction, comfort, and salvation of your subjects, above whom else shall never the Holy Ghost acknowledge that you rule in justice for their profit. If ye pretend to possess the kingdom with Christ Jesus, ye may not take example neither by the ignorant multitude of princes, neither by the ungodly and cruel rulers of the earth, of whom some pass their time in sloth, insolence, and riot without respect had to God's honor or to the salvation of their brethren, and other most cruelly oppress with Nimrod such as be subject to them. But your pattern and example must be the practice of those whom God hath approved by the testimony of his word, as after shall be declared.

Of the premises it is evident that to lawful powers is given the sword for punishment of malefactors, for maintenance of innocents, and for the profit and utility of their subjects. Now let us consider whether the reformation of religion fallen in decay and punishment of false teachers do appertain to the civil magistrate and nobility of any realm. I am not ignorant that Satan of old time for maintenance of his darkness hath obtained of the blind world two chief points: former, he hath persuaded to princes, rulers, and magistrates that the feeding of Christ's flock appertaineth nothing to their charge, but that it is rejected upon the bishops and estate ecclesiastical; and secondarily, that the reformation of religion, be it never so corrupt, and the punishment of such as be sworn soldiers in their kingdom are exempted from all civil power and are reserved to themselves and to their own cognition. But that no offender can justly be exempted from punishment and that the ordering and reformation of religion with the instruction of subjects doth especially appertain to the civil magistrate, shall God's perfect ordinance, his plain word, and the facts and examples of those that of God are highly praised, most evidently declare.

When God did establish his law, statutes, and ceremonies in the midst of Israel, he did not exempt the matters of religion from the power of Moses; but as he gave him charge over the civil polity, so he put in his mouth and in his hand, that is, he first revealed to him and thereafter commanded to put in practice whatsoever was to be taught or done in matters or religion. Nothing did God reveal particularly to Aaron, but altogether was he commanded to depend from the mouth of Moses.[22] Yea, nothing was he permitted to do himself or to his children either in his or their inauguration and sanctification to the priesthood, but all was committed to the care of Moses, and therefore were these words so frequently repeated to Moses: "Thou shalt separate Aaron and his sons from the midst of the people of Israel that they may execute the office of priesthood. Thou shalt make unto them garments, thou shalt annoint them, thou shalt wash them, thou shalt fill their hands with the sacrifice."[23] And so forth of every rite and ceremony that was to be done unto them, especial commandment was given unto Moses that he should do it. Now if Aaron and his sons were subject to Moses that they did nothing but at his commandment, who dare be so bold as to affirm that the civil magistrate hath nothing to do in matters of religion? For seeing that then God did so straitly require that even those who did bear the figure of Christ should receive from the civil power, as it were, their sanctification and entrance to their office, and seeing also that Moses was so far preferred to Aaron that the one commanded and the other did obey, who dare esteem that the civil power is now becomed so profane in God's eyes that it is sequestered from all intromission with the matters of religion.

The Holy Ghost in divers places declareth the contrary. For one of the chief precepts commanded to the king, when that he should be placed in his throne, was to write the example of the book of the Lord's law that it should be with him, that he might read in it all the days of his life, that he might learn to fear the Lord his God, and to keep all the words of his law, and his statutes to do them. This precept requireth not only that the king should himself fear God, keep his law and statutes, but that also he as the chief ruler should provide that God's true religion should be kept inviolated of the people and flock which by God was committed to his charge. And this did not only David and Solomon perfectly understand, but also some godly kings in Judah, after the apostasy and idolatry that infected Israel by the means of Jeroboam, did practice their understanding and execute their power in some notable reformations. For Asa and Jehoshaphat, Kings in Judah, finding the religion altogether corrupt, did apply their hearts, saith the Holy Ghost, to serve the Lord and to walk in his ways. And thereafter doth witness that Asa removed from honors his mother—some say grandmother—because she had committed and labored to maintain

horrible idolatry. And Jehoshaphat did not only refuse strange
gods himself, but also, destroying the chief monuments of idolatry, did send forth the Levites to instruct the people. Whereof it is
plain that the one and the other did understand such reformations
to appertain to their duties.[24]

But the facts of Hezekiah and of Josiah do more clearly prove
the power and duty of the civil magistrate in the reformation of
religion. Before the reign of Hezekiah so corrupt was the religion
that the doors of the house of the Lord were shut up, the lamps
were extinguished, no sacrifice was orderly made; but in the first
year of his reign, the first month of the same, did the King open
the doors of the temple, bring in the priests and Levites and,
assembling them together, did speak unto them as followeth:
"Hear me, O ye Levites, and be sanctified now, and sanctify also
the house of the Lord God of your fathers, and carry forth from
the sanctuary all filthiness" (he meaneth all monuments and vessels
of idolatry), "for our fathers have transgressed and have committed wickedness in the eyes of the eternal our God; they have
left him and have turned their faces from the tabernacle of the
Lord, and therefore is the wrath of the Lord comed upon Judah
and Jerusalem. Behold our fathers have fallen by the sword, our
sons, daughters, and wives are led in captivity, but now have I
purposed in my heart to make a covenant with the Lord God of
Israel that he may turn the wrath of his fury from us. And therefore, my sons," he sweetly exhorteth, "be not faint, for the Lord
hath chosen you to stand in his presence to serve him."[25]

Such as be not more than blind, clearly may perceive that the
King doth acknowledge that it appertained to his charge to reform
the religion, to appoint the Levites to their charge, and to admonish them of their duty and office; which thing he more evidently
declareth, writing his letters to all Israel, to Ephraim, and Manasseh and sent the same by the hands of messengers, having this
tenor: "You sons of Israel, return to the Lord God of Abraham,
Isaac, and Israel, and he shall return to the residue that resteth
from the hands of Assyria. Be not as yours and as your brethren
were, who have transgressed against the Lord God of their fathers,
who hath made them desolate as you see. Hold not your heart
therefore, but give your hand unto the Lord. Return unto his
sanctuary, serve him, and he shall shew mercy unto you, to your
sons and daughters that be in bondage, for he is pitiful and easy to
be entreated."[26]

Thus far did Hezekiah by letters and messengers provoke the

people, declined from God, to repentence, not only in Judah where he reigned lawful King but also in Israel, subject then to another King. And albeit that by some wicked men his messengers were mocked; yet as they lacked not their just punishment (for within six years after, Samaria was destroyed and Israel led captive by Shalmaneser), so did not the zealous King Hezekiah desist to prosecute his duty in restoring the religion of God's perfect ordinance, removing all abominations.

The same is to be read of Josiah, who did not only restore the religion but did further destroy all monuments of idolatry which of long time had remained.[27] For it is written of him that, after that the book of the Law was found and that he had asked counsel at the Prophetess Huldah, he sent and gathered all the elders of Judah and Jerusalem; and standing in the temple of the Lord, he made a covenant that all the people from the great to the small should walk after the Lord, should observe his law, statutes, and testimonies with all their heart and all their soul, and that they should ratify and confirm whatsoever was written in the book of God. He further commanded Helkiah the high priest and the priests of the inferior order that they should carry forth of the temple of the Lord all vessels that were made to Baal, which he burnt and did carry their powder to Bethel. He did further destroy all monuments of idolatry, yea, even those that had remained from the days of Solomon. He did burn them, stamp them to powder, whereof one part he scattered in the brook Kidron and the other upon the sepulchers and graves of the idolaters, whose bones he did burn upon the altars, where before they made sacrifice not only in Judah but also in Bethel, where Jeroboam had erected his idolatry. Yea, he further proceeded and did kill the priests of the high places, who were idolaters and had deceived the people; he did kill them, I say, and did burn their bones upon their own altars, and so returned to Jerusalem. This reformation made Josiah, and for the same obtained this testimony of the Holy Ghost that neither before him neither after him was there any such king who returned to God with his whole soul and with all his strength according to the law of Moses.[28]

Of which histories it is evident that the reformation of religion in all points, together with the punishment of false teachers doth appertain to the power of the civil magistrate. For what God required of them, his justice must require of others having the like charge and authority; what he did approve in them, he cannot but approve in all others who with like zeal and sincerity do enterprise to purge the Lord's temple and sanctuary. What God required of them it is before declared, to wit, that most diligently they should observe his law, statutes, and ceremonies, and how acceptable were their facts to God doth he himself witness. For to some he gave most notable victories without the hand of man, and in their most desperate dangers did declare his especial favors towards them by signs supernatural; to other he so established the kingdom that their enemies were compelled to stoop under their feet.[29] And the names of all he hath registered not only in the book of life but also in the blessed remembrance of all posterity since their days, which also shall continue till the coming of the Lord Jesus, who shall reward with the crown of immortality not only them but also such as unfeignedly study to do the will and to promote the glory of his heavenly father in the midst of this corrupted generation. In consideration whereof ought you, my lords, all delay set apart to provide for the reformation of religion in your dominions and bounds, which now is so corrupt that no part of Christ's institution remaineth in the original purity; and therefore of necessity it is that speedily ye provide for reformation of else ye declare yourselves not only void of love towards your subjects but also to live without care of your own salvation, yea, without all fear and true reverence of God.

Two things perchance may move you to esteem these histories, before briefly touched, to appertain nothing to you. First, because you are no Jews but gentiles, and secondarily, because you are no kings but nobles in your realm. But be not deceived. For neither of both can excuse you in God's presence from doing your duty, for it is a thing more than certain that, whatsoever God required of the civil magistrate in Israel or Judah, concerning the observation of true religion during the time of the Law, the same doth he require of lawful magistrates, professing Christ Jesus in the time of the Gospel, as the Holy Ghost hath taught us by the mouth of David, saying, Psalm 2, "Be learned you that judge the earth, kiss the son, lest that the Lord wax angry and that ye perish from the way." This admonition did not extend to the judges under the Law only but doth also include all such as be promoted to honors in the time of the Gospel, when Christ Jesus doth reign and fight in his spiritual kingdom, whose enemies in that Psalm be first most sharply taxed, their fury expressed, and vanity mocked. And then are kings and judges, who think themselves free from all law and obedience, commanded to repent their former blind rage, and judges are charged to be learned; and last are all commanded to serve the eternal in fear, to rejoice before him in trembling, to kiss the son, that is, to give unto him most humble obedience, whereof it is evident that the rulers, magistrates, and judges now in Christ's kingdom are no less bound to obedience unto God than were those under the Law.

And how is it possible that any shall be obedient who despise his religion, in which standeth the chief glory that man can give to God and is a service which God especially requireth of kings and rulers? Which thing St. Augustine plainly did note, writing to one Bonifacius, a man of war, according to the same argument and purpose which I labor to persuade your honors. For after that he hath in that his epistle declared the difference betwixt the heresy of the Donatists and Arians and hath somewhat spoken of their cruelty, he sheweth the way how their fury should and ought to be repressed and that it is lawful for the injustly afflicted to seek support and defense at godly magistrates. For thus he writeth: "Either must the verity be kept close, or else must their cruelty be sustained. But if the verity should be concealed, not only should none be saved nor delivered by such silence, but also should many be lost through their decept. But if by preaching of the verity their fury should be provoked more to rage, and by that means yet some were delivered, yet should fear hinder many weaklings to follow the verity, if their rage be not stayed."

In these first words Augustine sheweth three reasons why the afflicted church in those days called for the help of the emperor and of godly magistrates against the fury of the persecutors. The first, the verity must be spoken, or else mankind shall perish in error. The second, the verity, being plainly spoken, provoketh the adversaries to rage. And because that some did allege that rather we ought to suffer all injury than to seek support by man, he addeth the third reason, to wit, that many weak ones be not able to suffer persecution and death for the truth's sake, to whom not the less respect ought to be had that they may be won from error and so be brought to greater strength.

O that rulers of this age should ponder and weigh the reasons of this godly writer and provide the remedy which he requireth in these words following: "Now when the church was thus afflicted if any think that rather they should have sustained all calamity than that the help of God should have been asked by Christian Emperors, he doth not well advert that of such negligence no good compts or reason could be given. For where such as would that no just laws should be made against their impiety allege that the Apostles sought no such things of the kings of the earth, they do not consider that then the time was other than it is now, and that all things are done in their own time. What emperor then believed in Christ that should serve him in making laws for godliness against impiety? While yet that saying of the prophet was complete, 'Why hath nations raged, and people have imagined vanity? The kings of the earth have stand up, and princes have convented together against the Lord and against his annointed,' that which is after said in the same Psalm was not yet come to pass: 'And now understand, O you kings, be learned you that judge the earth serve the Lord in fear and rejoice to him with trembling.' How do kings serve the Lord in fear but in punishing and by a godly severity forbidding those things which are done against the commandment of the Lord. For otherwise doth he serve insofar as he is man, otherwise insofar as he is king. Insofar as he is man, he serveth him by living faithfully; but because he is also king, he serveth, establishing laws that command the things that be just and that with a convenient rigor forbid things contrary. As Hezekiah served, destroying the groves, the temples of idols, and the places which were builded against God's commandment; so served also Josiah, doing the same; so served the King of Ninevites, compelling the whole city to mitigate the Lord; so served Darius, giving in the power of Daniel the idol to be broken and his enemies to be cast to the lions; so served Nebuchadnezzar by a terrible law, forbidding all that were in his realm to blaspheme God. Herein therefore do kings serve the Lord insofar as they are kings when they do those things to serve him which none except kings be able to do."[30] He further proceedeth and concludeth that, as when wicked kings do reign, impiety cannot be bridled by laws but rather is tyranny exercised under the title of the same, so it is a thing without all reason that kings, professing the knowledge and honor of God, should not regard nor care who did defend nor who did oppugn the church of God in their dominions.

By these words of this ancient and godly writer, your honors may perceive what I require of you, to wit, to repress the tyranny of your bishops and to defend the innocents professing the truth. He did require of the emperor and kings of his days, professing Christ, and manifestly concludeth that they cannot serve Christ except that so they do. Let not your bishops think that Augustine speaketh for them because he nameth the church. Let them read and understand that Augustine writeth for that church which professeth the truth and doth suffer persecution for the defense of the same, which your bishops do not, but rather with the Donatists and Arians do cruelly persecute all such as boldly speak Christ's eternal verity to manifest their impiety and abomination. But thus much we have of Augustine that it appertaineth to the obedience and service which kings owe to God, as well now in the time of the Gospel as before under the Law, to defend the afflicted for matters of religion and repress the fury of the persecutors by the rigor and severity of godly laws. For which cause, no doubt, doth Isaiah the Prophet say that, "kings should be nourishers to the church of God, that they should abase their heads, and lovingly embrace the children of God."[31] And thus, I say, your honors may evidently see that the same obedience doth God require of rulers and princes in the time of the Gospel that he required in the time of the Law.

If you do think that the reformation of religion and defense of the afflicted doth not appertain to you because you are no kings but nobles and estates of a realm, in two things you are deceived. Former, in that you do not advert that David requireth as well that the princes and judges of the earth be learned and that they serve and fear God, as that he requireth that the kings repent. If you therefore be judges and princes, as no man can deny you to be, then by the plain words of David you are charged to be learned, to serve and fear God, which ye cannot do if you despise the reformation of his religion. And this is your first error.

The second is that ye neither know your duty which ye owe to God, neither yet your authority which of him ye have received, if ye for pleasure or fear of any earthly man despise God's true religion and contemn your brethren that in his name call for your support. Your duty is to hear the voice of the eternal, your God, and unfeignedly to study to follow his precepts, who, as is before said, of especial mercy hath promoted you to honors and dignity. His chief and principal precept is that with reverence ye receive and embrace his only beloved son Jesus, that ye promote to the uttermost of your powers his true religion, and that ye defend your brethren and subjects whom he hath put under your charge and care.

Now, if your king be a man ignorant of God, enemy to his true religion, blinded by superstition, and a persecutor of Christ's members, shall ye be excused if with silence ye pass over his iniquity? Be not deceived, my lords, ye are placed in authority for another purpose than to flatter your king in his folly and blind rage, to wit, that as with your bodies, strength, riches, and wisdom ye are bound to assist and defend him in all things which by your advice he shall take in hand for God's glory and for the preservation of his commonwealth and subjects, so by your gravities, counsel, and admonition ye are bound to correct and repress whatsoever ye know him to attempt expressedly repugning to God's word, honor, and glory, or what ye shall espy him to do, be it by ignorance or be it by malice, against his subjects great or small. Of which last part of your obedience if ye defraud your king, ye commit against him no less treason than if ye did extract from him your due and promised support what time by his enemies injustly he were pursued.

But this part of their duty, I fear, do a small number of the nobility of this age rightly consider; neither yet will they understand that for that purpose hath God promoted them. For now the common song of all men is, we must obey our kings, be they good or be they bad, for God hath so commanded. But horrible shall the vengeance be that shall be poured forth upon such blasphemers of God, his holy name, and ordinance. For it is no less blasphemy to say that God hath commanded kings to be obeyed when they command impiety than to say that God by his precept is author and maintainer of all iniquity. True it is God hath commanded kings to be obeyed, but like true it is that in things which they commit against his glory, or when cruelly without cause they rage against their brethren the members of Christ's body, he hath commanded no obedience, but rather he hath approved, yea, and greatly rewarded such as have opponed themselves to their ungodly commandments and blind rage, as in the examples of the three children, of Daniel, and Ebedmelech it is evident.

The three children would neither bow nor stoop before the golden image at the commandment of the great King Nebuchadnezzar. Daniel did openly pray, his windows being open, against the established law of Darius and of his council. And Ebedmelech feared not to enter in before the presence of Zedekiah and boldly to defend the cause and innocency of Jeremiah the Prophet, whom the King and his council had condemned to death.[32] Every one of these facts should this day be judged foolish by such as will not understand what confession God doth require of his children when his verity is oppugned or his glory called in doubt; such men, I say, as prefer man to God and things present to the heavenly inheritance, should have judged every one of these facts stubborn inobedience, foolish presumption and singularity, or else bold controlling of the king and his wise council. But how acceptable in God's presence was this resistance to the ungodly commandments and determinations of their king, the end did witness. For the three children were delivered from the furnace of fire and Daniel from the den of lions to the confusion of their enemies, to better instruction of the ignorant king, and to the perpetual comfort of God's afflicted children.

And Ebedmelech, in the day of the Lord's visitation when the King and his council did drink the bitter cup of God's vengeance, did find his life for a prey and did not fall in the edge of the sword when many thousands did perish. And this was signified unto him by the Prophet himself at the commandment of God before that Jerusalem was destroyed. The promise and cause were recited unto him in these words: "I will bring my words upon this city unto evil and not unto good, but most assuredly I shall deliver thee because thou hast trusted in me, saith the Lord." The trust and hope which Ebedmelech had in God made him bold to oppone himself, being but one, to the King and to his whole council who had condemned to death the Prophet, whom his conscience did acknowledge to be innocent. For this did he speak in the presence of the King, sitting in the port of Benjamin: "My Lord, the King," saith Ebedmelech, "these men do wickedly in all things that they have done to Jeremiah the Prophet."[33]

Advert and take heed, my lords, that the men who had condemned the Prophet were the King, his princes, and council, and yet did one man accuse them all of iniquity and did boldly speak in the defense of him whose innocence he was persuaded. And the same, I say, is the duty of every man in his vocation, but chiefly of the nobility which is joined with their kings to bridle and repress their folly and blind rage. Which thing, if the nobility do not neither yet labor to do, as they are traitors to their kings, so do they provoke the wrath of God against themselves and against the realm in which they abuse the authority which they have received of God to maintain virtue and to repress vice. For hereof I would your honors were most certainly persuaded that God will neither excuse nobility nor people, but the nobility least of all, that obey and follow their kings in manifest iniquity; but with the same vengeance will God punish the prince, people, and nobility, conspiring together against him and his holy ordinances, as in the punishment taken upon Pharaoh, Israel, Judah, and Babylon is evidently to be seen. For Pharaoh was not drowned alone, but his captains, chariots, and great army drank the same cup with him. The kings of Israel and Judah were not punished without company, but with them were murdered the councillors, their princes imprisoned, and their people led captive. And why? Because none was found so faithful to God that he durst enterprise to resist nor againststand the manifest impiety of their princes. And therefore was God's wrath poured forth upon the one and the other. But the more ample discourse of this argument I defer to better opportunity; only at this time I thought expedient to admonish you that before God it shall not excuse you to allege, we are no kings and therefore neither can we reform religion nor yet defend such as be persecuted. Consider, my lords, that ye are powers ordained by God, as is before declared; and therefore doth the reformation of religion and the defense of such as injustly are oppressed appertain to your charge and care, which thing shall the law of God, universally given to be kept of all men, most evidently declare, which is my last and most assured reason why I say ye ought to remove from honors and to punish with death such as God hath condemned by his own mouth.

After that Moses had declared what was true religion, to wit, to honor God as he commanded, adding nothing to his word, neither yet diminishing anything from it, after also that vehemently he had exhorted the same law to be observed, he denounceth the punishment against the transgressors in these words:[34] "If thy brother, son, daughter, wife, or neighbor, whom thou lovest as thine own life, solicitate thee secretly, saying, let us go serve other gods whom neither thou nor thy fathers have known, consent not to hear him, hear him not, let not thine eye spare him, shew him no indulgency or favor, hide him not, but utterly kill him; let thy hand be the first upon him that he may be slain, and after the hand of the whole people."[35] Of these words of Moses are two things appertaining to our purpose to be noted. Former, that such as solicitate only to idolatry ought to be punished to death without favor or respect of person. For he that will not suffer man to spare his son, his daughter, nor his wife, but straitly commandeth punishment to be taken upon the idolaters—have they never so nigh conjunction with us—will not wink at the idolatry of others of what estate or condition soever they be.

It is not unknown that the Prophets had revelations of God which were not common to the people, as Samuel had the revelation that Eli and his posterity should be destroyed, that Saul should first be king and thereafter that he should be rejected, that David should reign for him.[36] Micaiah understood by vision that Ahab should be killed in battle against the Syrians.[37] Elijah saw that dogs should eat Jezebel in the fortress of Jezreel.[38] Elisha did see hunger come upon Israel by the space of seven years.[39] Jeremiah did foresee the destruction of Jerusalem and the time of their captivity, and so divers other Prophets had divers revelations of God which the people did not otherwise understand but by their affirmation; and therefore in those days were the Prophets named seers, because that God did open unto them that which was hid from the multitude. Now if any man might have claimed any privilege from the rigor of the law or might have justified his fact, it should have been the Prophet. For he might have alleged for himself his singular prerogative that he had above other men to have God's will revealed unto him by vision or by dream, or that God had declared particularly unto him that his pleasure was to be honored in that manner, in such a place, and by such means. But all such excuses doth God remove, commanding that the Prophet that shall solicitate the people to serve strange gods shall die the death, notwithstanding that he allege for himself dream, vision, or revelation. Yea, although he promise miracles and also that such things as he promiseth come to pass, yet, I say, commandeth God that no credit be given to him, but that he die the death, because he teacheth apostasy and defection from God.

Hereof your honors may easily espy that none provoking the people to idolatry ought to be exempted from the punishment of death. For if neither that inseparable conjunction which God himself hath sanctified betwixt man and wife, neither that unspeakable love grafted in nature which is betwixt the father and the son, neither yet that reverence which God's people ought to bear to the Prophets, can excuse any man to spare the offender or to conceal his offense, what excuse can man pretend which God will accept? Evident it is that no estate, condition, nor honor can exempt the idolater from the hands of God when he shall call him to accompts or shall inflict punishment upon him for his offense; how shall it then excuse the people that they, according to God's commandment, punish not to death such as shall solicitate or violently draw the people to idolatry? And this is the first which I would your honors should note of the former words, to wit, that no person is exempted from punishment if he can be manifestly convicted to have provoked or led the people to idolatry. And this is most evidently declared in that solemn oath and covenant which Asa made with the people to serve God and to maintain his religion, adding this penalty to the transgressors of it, to wit, that "whosoever should not seek the Lord God of Israel should be killed, were he great or were he small, were it man or were it woman."[40] And of this oath was the Lord compleased; he was fond of them and gave them rest on every part, because they sought him with their whole heart and did swear to punish the offenders according to the precept of his law, without respect of persons. And this is it which, I say, I would your honors should note for the first: that no idolater can be exempted from punishment by God's law.

The second is that the punishment of such crimes as are idolatry, blasphemy, and others that touch the majesty of God doth not appertain to kings and chief rulers only but also to the whole body of that people and to every member of the same, according to the vocation of every man and according to that possibility and occasion which God doth minister to revenge the injury done against his glory what time that impiety is manifestly known. And that doth Moses more plainly speak in these words: "If in any of thy cities," saith he, "which the Lord thy God giveth unto thee to dwell in them, thou shalt hear this bruit: there are some men, the sons of Belial, passed forth from thee and have solicited the citizens of their cities by these words: let us go and serve strange gods which you have not known, search and inquire diligently; and if it be true that such abomination is done in the midst of thee, thou shalt utterly strike the inhabitants of that city with the sword, thou shalt destroy it and whatsoever is within it, thou shalt gather the spoil of it in the midst of the marketplace, thou shalt burn that city with fire and the spoil of it to the Lord thy God that it may be a heap of stones forever, neither shall it be any more builded. Let nothing of that execration cleave to thy hand that the Lord may turn from the fury of his wrath and be moved towards thee with inward affection."[41] Plain it is that Moses speaketh nor giveth not charge to kings, rulers, and judges only, but he commandeth the whole body of the people, yea, and every member of the same according to their possibility.

And who dare to be so impudent as to deny this to be most reasonable and just? For, seeing that God had delivered the whole body from bondage, and to the whole multitude had given his law, and to the twelve tribes had he so distributed the inheritance of the land of Canaan that no family could complain that it was neglected, was not the whole and every member addebted to confess and acknowledge the benefits of God, yea, had it not been the part of every man to have studied to keep the possession which he had received? Which thing God did plainly pronounce they should not do, except that in their hearts they did sanctify the Lord God, that they embraced and inviolably kept his religion established, and finally except they did cut out iniquity from amongst them, declaring themselves earnest enemies to those abominations which God declared himself so vehemently to hate that first he commanded the whole inhabitants of that country to be destroyed and all monuments of their idolatry to be broken down, and thereafter he also straitly commandeth that a city declining to idolatry should fall in the edge of the sword, and that the whole spoil of the same should be burned, no portion of it reserved.[42]

To the carnal man this may appear a rigorous and severe judgment, yea, it may rather seem to be pronounced in a rage than in wisdom. For what city was ever yet in which, to man's judgment, were not to be found many innocent persons, as infants, children, and some simple and ignorant souls who neither did nor could consent to such impiety? And yet we find no exception, but all are appointed to the cruel death. And as concerning the city and the spoil of the same, man's reason cannot think but that it might have been better bestowed than to be consumed with fire and so profit no man. But in such cases will God that all creatures stoop, cover their faces, and desist from reasoning when commandment is given to execute his judgment.

Albeit I could adduce divers causes of such severity, yet will I search none other than the Holy Ghost hath assigned. First, that all Israel, hearing the judgment, should fear to commit the like abomination; and secondarily, that the Lord might turn from the fury of his anger, might be moved towards the people with inward affection, be merciful unto them, and multiply them according to his oath made unto their fathers. Which reasons, as they are sufficient in God's children to correct the murmuring of the grudging flesh, so ought they to provoke every man, as before I have said, to declare himself enemy to that which so highly provoketh the wrath of God against the whole people. For where Moses saith, "let the city be burned, and let no part of the spoil cleave to thy hand that the Lord may return from the fury of his wrath," etc., he plainly doth signify that by the defection and idolatry of a few God's wrath is kindled against the whole, which is never quenched till such punishment be taken upon the offenders: that whatsoever served them in their idolatry be brought to destruction, because that it is execrable and accursed before God. And therefore he will not that it be reserved for any use of his people.

I am not ignorant that this law was not put in execution as God commanded; but what did thereof ensue and follow histories declare, to wit, plague after plague till Israel and Judah were led in captivity, as the Books of Kings do witness. The consideration whereof maketh me more bold to affirm that it is the duty of every man that list to escape the plague and punishments of God to declare himself enemy to idolatry not only in heart, hating the same, but also in external gesture, declaring that he lamenteth, if he can do no more, for such abominations. Which thing was shewed to the Prophet Ezekiel what time he gave him to understand why he would destroy Judah with Israel, and that he would remove his glory from the temple and place that he had chosen, and so pour forth his wrath and indignation upon the city that was full of blood and apostasy—which became so impudent that it durst be bold to say, "the Lord hath left the earth and seeth not." At this time, I say, the Lord revealed in vision to his Prophet who they were that should find favor in that miserable destruction, to wit, "those that did mourn and lament for all the abominations done in the city, in whose foreheads did God command to print and seal Tau" to the end that the destroyer, who was commanded to strike the rest without mercy, should not hurt them in whom the sign was found.[43]

Of these premises I suppose it be evident that the punishment of idolatry doth not appertain to kings only but also to the whole people, yea, to every member of the same according to his possibility. For that is a thing most assured that no man can mourn, lament, and bewail for those things which he will not remove to the uttermost of his power. If this be required of the whole people and of every man in his vocation, what shall be required of you, my lords, whom God hath raised up to be princes and rulers above your brethren, whose hands he hath armed with the sword of his justice, yea, whom he hath appointed to be as bridles to repress the rage and insolency of your kings whensoever they pretend manifestly to transgress God's blessed ordinance?

If any think that this my affirmation, touching the punishment of idolaters, be contrary to the practice of the Apostles who, finding the gentiles in idolatry, did call them to repentance, requiring no such punishment, let the same man understand that the gentiles, before the preaching of Christ, lived, as the Apostle speaketh, without God in the world, drowned in idolatry, according to the blindness and ignorance in which then they were holden, as a profane nation, whom God had never openly avowed to be his people, had never received in his household, neither given unto them laws to be kept in religion nor polity; and therefore did not

his Holy Ghost, calling them to repentance, require of them any
corporal punishment according to the rigor of the law unto the
which they were never subjects, as they that were strangers from
the commonwealth of Israel.[44] But if any think that, after that the
gentiles were called from their vain conversation, and, by embracing Christ, were received in the number of Abraham's children,
and so made one people with the Jews believing, if any think, I say,
that then they were not bound to the same obedience which God
required of his people Israel what time he confirmed his league and
covenant with them, the same man appeareth to make Christ inferior to Moses and contrarious to the law of his heavenly father.
For if the contempt or transgression of Moses' law was worthy of
death, what should we judge the contempt of Christ's ordinance to
be (I mean after they be once received)? And if Christ be not
comed to dissolve but to fulfill the world of his heavenly father,
shall the liberty of his Gospel be an occasion that the especial glory
of his father be trodden underfoot and regarded of no man? God
forbid.

The especial glory of God is that such as profess them to be his
people should hearken to his voice; and amongst all the voices of
God revealed to the world, touching punishment of vices, is none
more evident neither more severe than is that which is pronounced
against idolatry, the teachers and maintainers of the same.[45] And
therefore I fear not to affirm that the gentiles (I mean every city,
realm, province, or nation amongst the gentiles, embracing Christ
Jesus and his true religion) be bound to the same league and covenant that God made with his people Israel what time he promised
to root out nations before them in these words: "Beware that thou
make any covenant with the inhabitants of the land to the which
thou comest, lest perchance, that this come in ruin, that is, be
destruction to thee; but thou shalt destroy their altars, break their
idols, and cut down their groves. Fear no strange gods, worship
them not, neither yet make you sacrifice to them. But the Lord,
who in his greater power and outstretched arm hath brought you
out of the land of Egypt, shall you fear, him shall you honor, him
shall you worship, to him shall you make sacrifice; his statutes,
judgments, laws, and commandments you shall keep and observe.
This is the covenant which I have made with you, saith the Eternal,
forget it not, neither yet fear ye other gods; but fear you the Lord
your God, and he shall deliver you from the hands of all your
enemies."[46]

To this same law, I say, and covenant are the gentiles no less bound than sometimes were the Jews. Whensoever God doth illuminate the eyes of any multitude, province, people or city and putteth the sword in their own hand to remove such enormities from amongst them as, before God, they know to be abominable, then, I say, are they no less bound to purge their dominions, cities, and countries from idolatry than were the Israelites what time they received the possession of the land of Canaan. And moreover, I say, if any go about to erect and set up idolatry or to teach defection from God after that the verity hath been received and approved, that then, not only the magistrates to whom the sword is committed, but also the people are bound by that oath which they have made to God to revenge to the uttermost of their power the injury done against his majesty.

In universal defections and in a general revolt, such as was in Israel after Jeroboam, there is a diverse consideration. For then because the whole people were together conspired against God, there could none be found that would execute the punishment which God had commanded till God raised up Jehu, whom he had appointed for that purpose. And the same is to be considered in all other general defections, such as this day be in the papistry where all are blinded and all are declined from God, and that of long continuance, so that no ordinary justice can be executed, but the punishment must be reserved to God and unto such means as he shall appoint.

But I do speak of such a number as, after they have received God's perfect religion, do boldly profess the same, notwithstanding that some or the most part fall back, as of late days was in England; unto such a number, I say, it is lawful to punish the idolaters with death, if by any means God give them the power. For so did Joshua and Israel determine to have done against the children of Reuben, Gad, and Manasseh for their suspect apostasy and defection from God. And the whole tribes did in very deed execute the sharp judgment against the tribe of Benjamin for a less offense than for idolatry. And the same ought to be done wheresoever Christ Jesus and his Evangel is so received in any realm, province, or city that the magistrates and people have solemnly avowed and promised to defend the same, as under King Edward of late days was done in England. In such places, I say, it is not only lawful to punish to the death such as labor to subvert the true religion, but the magistrates and people are bound so to do unless they will provoke the wrath of God against themselves. And therefore I fear not to affirm that it had been the duty of the nobility,

judges, rulers, and people of England not only to have resisted and
againststanded Mary, that Jezebel whom they call their Queen, but
also to have punished her to the death with all the sort of her
idolatrous priests together with all such as should have assisted her
what time that she and they openly began to suppress Christ's
Evangel, to shed the blood of the saints of God, and to erect that
most devilish idolatry—the papistical abominations and his
usurped tyranny, which once most justly by common oath was
banished from that realm.

But because I cannot at this present discuss this argument as it
appertaineth, I am compelled to omit it to better opportunity; and
so, returning to your honors, I say that if ye confess yourselves
baptised in the Lord Jesus, of necessity ye must confess that the
care of his religion doth appertain to your charge. And if ye know
that in your hands God hath put the sword for the causes above
expressed, then can ye not deny but that the punishment of obstinate and malapert idolaters, such as all your bishops be, doth
appertain to your office, if after admonition they continue obstinate.

I am not ignorant what be the vain defenses of your proud
prelates. They claim first a prerogative and privilege that they are
exempted, and that by consent of councils and emperors, from all
jurisdiction of the temporality. And secondarily, when they are
convicted of manifest impieties, abuses, and enormities—as well in
their manners as in religion, neither fear nor shame they to affirm
that things so long established cannot suddenly be reformed, although they be corrupted; but with process of time they promise
to take order. But in a few words I answer that no privilege granted
against the ordinance and statutes of God is to be observed, although all councils and men in the earth have appointed the same.
But against God's ordinance it is that idolaters, murderers, false
teachers, and blasphemers shall be exempted from punishment, as
before is declared; and therefore in vain it is that they claim for
privilege when that God saith, "the murderer shalt thou rive from
my altar that he may die the death." And as to the order and
reformation which they promise, that is to be looked or hoped for
when Satan, whose children and slaves they are, can change his
nature. This answer, I doubt not, shall suffice the sober and godly
reader.

But yet to the end that they may further see their own confusion
and that your honors may better understand what ye ought to do
in so manifest a corruption and defection from God, I ask of

themselves what assurance they have for this their immunity, exemption, or privilege? Who is the author of it, and what fruit it hath produced?

And first I say that of God they have no assurance neither yet can he be proved to be author of any such privilege. But the contrary is easy to be seen. For God, in establishing his orders in Israel, did so subject Aaron (in his priesthood being the figure of Christ) to Moses that he feared not to call him in judgment and to constrain him to give accompt of his wicked deed in consenting to idolatry, as the history doth plainly witness. For thus it is written: "Then Moses took the calf which they had made, and burned it with fire, and did grind it to powder, and scattering it in the water, gave it to drink to the children of Israel" (declaring hereby the vanity of their idol and the abomination of the same); and thereafter, "Moses said to Aaron, 'what hath this people done to thee that thou shouldst bring upon it so great a sin?' "[47] Thus, I say, doth Moses call and accuse Aaron of the destruction of the whole people, and yet he perfectly understood that God had appointed him to be the high priest that he should bear upon his shoulders and upon his breast the names of the twelve tribes of Israel, for whom he was appointed to make sacrifice, prayers, and supplications. He knew his dignity was so great that only he might enter within the most holy place, but neither could his office nor dignity exempt him from judgment when he had offended.

If any object Aaron at that time was not anointed and therefore was he subject to Moses, I have answered that Moses, being taught by the mouth of God, did perfectly understand to what dignity Aaron was appointed, and yet he feared not to call him in judgment and to compel him to make answer for his wicked fact. But if this answer doth not suffice, yet shall the Holy Ghost witness further in the matter.

Solomon removed from honor Abiathar, being the high priest, and commanded him to cease from all function and to live as a private man. Now if the unction did exempt the priest from jurisdiction of the civil magistrate, Solomon did offend, and injured Abiathar. For he was anointed and had carried the ark before David. But God doth not reprove the fact of Solomon, neither yet doth Abiathar claim any prerogative by the reason of his office; but rather doth the Holy Ghost approve the fact of Solomon, saying, "Solomon ejected forth Abiathar that he should not be the priest of the Lord, that the word of the Lord might be performed which he spake unto the house of Eli." And Abiathar did think that he obtained great favor in that he did escape the present death which by his conspiracy he had deserved.[48] If any yet reason that Abiathar was no otherwise subject to the judgment of the King, but as he was appointed to be the executor of that sentence which God before had pronounced, as I will not greatly deny that reason, so require I that every man consider that the same God who pronounced sentence against Eli and his house hath pronounced also that idolaters, whoremongers, murderers, and blasphemers shall neither have portion in the kingdom of God neither ought to be permitted to bear any rule in his church and congregation.[49]

Now if the unction and office saved not Abiathar, because that God's sentence must needs be performed, can any privilege granted by man be a buckler to malefactors that they shall not be subject to the punishments pronounced by God? I think no man will be so foolish as so to affirm. For a thing more than evident it is that the whole priesthood in the time of the Law was bound to give obedience to the civil powers. And if any member of the same was found criminal, the same was subject to the punishment of the sword which God had put in the hand of the magistrate.

And this ordinance of his father did not Christ disannul but rather did confirm the same, commanding tribute to be paid for himself and for Peter, who, perfectly knowing the mind of his master, thus writeth in his Epistle: "Submit yourselves to all manner ordinance of man" (he excepteth such as be expressly repugning to God's commandment) "for the Lord's sake, whether it be to king as to the chief head, or unto rulers as unto them that are sent by him for punishment of evil doers and for the praise of them that do well."[50] The same doth the Apostle St. Paul most plainly command in these words: "Let every soul be subject to the superior powers."[51] Which places make evident that neither Christ neither his Apostles hath given any assurance of this immunity and privilege which men of church, as they will be termed, do this day claim.

Yea, it was a thing unknown to the primitive church many years after the days of the Apostles. For Chrysostom, who served in the church at Constantinople four hundred years after Christ's ascension and after that corruption was greatly increased, doth yet thus write upon the foresaid words of the Apostle: "This precept," saith he, "doth not appertain to such as be called seculars only but even to those that be priests and religious men." And after he addeth: "Whether thou be Apostle, Evangelist, Prophet, or whosoever thou be thou canst not be exempted from this subjection."[52]

Hereof it is plain that Chrysostom did not understand that God had exempted any person from obedience and subjection of the civil power, neither yet that he was author of such exemption and privilege, as papists do this day claim. And the same was the judgment and uniform doctrine of the primitive church many years after Christ.

Your honors do wonder, I doubt not, from what fountain then did this their immunity, as they term it, and singular privilege spring. I shall shortly touch that which is evident in their own laws and histories. When the Bishops of Rome, the very Antichrists, had, partly by fraud and partly by violence, usurped the superiority of some places in Italy, and most injustly had spoiled the emperors of their rents and possessions, and had also murdered some of their officers—as histories do witness, then began pope after pope to practice and devise how they should be exempted from judgment of princes and from equity of laws. And in this point they were most vigilant, till at length iniquity did so prevail in their hands, according as Daniel had before prophesied of them, that this sentence was pronounced: "Neither by the emperor, neither by the clergy, neither yet by the people shall the judge be judged." "God will," saith Symmachus, "that the causes of others be determined by men, but without all question he hath reserved the bishop of this seat" (understanding Rome) "to his own judgment."[53] And hereof divers popes and expositors of their laws would seem to give reasons, for, saith Agatho, "all the precepts of the apostolic seat are assured as by the voice of God himself."[54] The author of the gloss upon their canon affirmeth that if all the world should pronounce sentence against the pope, yet should his sentence prevail, for, saith he: "The pope hath a heavenly will, and therefore he may change the nature of things; he may apply the substance of one thing to another, and of nothing he may make somewhat; and that sentence which was nothing, that is, by his mind false and injust, he may make somewhat that is true and just." "For," saith he, "in all things that please him his will is for reason. Neither is there any man that may ask of him, why dost thou so. For he may dispense above the law, and of injustice he may make justice. For he hath the fullness of all power."[55] And many other most blasphemous sentences did they pronounce every one after other, which for shortness sake I omit, till at the end they obtained this most horrible decree: that albeit in life and conversation they were so wicked and detestable that not only they condemned themselves but that also they drew to hell and perdition many thousands with them, yet that none should presume to reprehend or rebuke them.[56]

This being established for the head (albeit not without some contradiction, for some emperors did require due obedience of them, as God's word commanded and ancient bishops had given before to emperors and to their laws; but Satan so prevailed in his suit before the blind world that the former sentences were confirmed, which power being granted to the head), then began provision to be made for the rest of the members in all realms and countries where they made residence. The fruit whereof we see to be this: that none of that pestilent generation—I mean the vermin of the papistical order—will be subject to any civil magistrate how enormous that ever his crime be, but will be reserved to their own ordinary, as they term it.

And what fruits have hereof ensued, be the world never so blind, it cannot but witness. For how their head, that Roman Antichrist, hath been occupied ever since the granting of such privileges histories do witness, and of late the most part of Europa, subject to the plague of God, to fire and sword by his procurement, hath felt and this day doth feel. The pride, ambition, envy, excess, fraud, spoil, oppression, murder, filthy life, and incest that is used and maintained among that rabble of priests, friars, monks, canons, bishops, and cardinals cannot be expressed. I fear not to affirm, neither doubt I to prove, that the papistical church is further degenerate from the purity of Christ's doctrine, from the footsteps of the Apostles, and from the manners of the primitive church than was the church of the Jews from God's holy statutes what time it did crucify Christ Jesus, the only Messiah, and most cruelly persecute his Apostles.

And yet will our papists claim their privileges and ancient liberties, which, if you grant unto them, my lords, ye shall assuredly drink the cup of God's vengeance with them and shall be reputed before his presence companions of thieves and maintainers of murderers, as is before declared. For their immunity and privilege, whereof so greatly they boast, is nothing else but as if thieves, murderers, or brigands should conspire amongst themselves that they would never answer in judgment before any lawful magistrate to the end that their theft and murder should not be punished; even such, I say, is their wicked privilege which neither they have of God the father, neither of Christ Jesus who hath revealed his father's will to the world, neither yet of the Apostles, nor primitive church, as before is declared. But it is a thing conspired amongst themselves to the end that their iniquity, detestable life, and tyranny shall neither be repressed nor reformed.

And if they object that godly emperors did grant and confirm the same, I answer that the godliness of no man is or can be of sufficient authority to justify a foolish and ungodly fact—such, I mean, as God hath not allowed by his word. For Abraham was a godly man, but the denial of his wife was such a fact as no godly man ought to imitate. The same I might shew of David, Hezekiah, and Josiah, unto whom I think no man of judgment will prefer any emperor since Christ in holiness and wisdom; and yet are not all their facts, not even such as they appeared to have done for good causes, to be approved nor followed. And therefore, I say, as error and ignorance remain always with the most perfect man in his life, so must their works be examined by another rule than by their own holiness, if they shall be approved.

But if this answer doth not suffice, then will I answer more shortly that no godly emperor since Christ's ascension hath granted any such privilege to any such church or person as they— the whole generation of papists—be at this day. I am not ignorant that some emperors of a certain zeal and for some considerations granted liberties to the true church afflicted, for their maintenance against tyrants. But what serveth this for the defense of their tyranny? If the law must be understanded according to the mind of the lawgiver, then must they first prove themselves Christ's true and afflicted church before they can claim any privilege to appertain to them. For only to that church were the privileges granted. It will not be their glorious titles, neither yet the long possession of the name that can prevail in this so weighty a cause. For all those had the church of Jerusalem which did crucify Christ and did condemn his doctrine.

We offer to prove by their fruits and tyranny, by the Prophets, and plain Scriptures of God what trees and generation they be, to wit, unfruitful and rotten, apt for nothing but to be cut and cast in hell fire, yea, that they are the very kingdom of Antichrist, of whom we are commanded to be beware. And therefore, my lords, to return to you, seeing that God hath armed your hands with the sword of justice, seeing that his law most straitly commandeth idolaters and false prophets to be punished with death, and that you be placed above your subjects to reign as fathers over their children, and further seeing that not only I but with me many thousand famous, godly, and learned persons accuse your bishops and the whole rabble of the papistical clergy of idolatry, of murder, and of blasphemy against God committed, it appertaineth to your honors to be vigilant and careful in so weighty a matter. The question is not of earthly substance but of the glory of God and of the salvation of yourselves and of your brethren subject to your charge, in which, if you after this plain admonition be negligent, there resteth no excuse by reason of ignorance. For in the name of God I require of you that the cause of religion may be tried in your presence by the plain and simple word of God, that your bishops be compelled to desist from their tyranny, that they be compelled to make answer for the neglecting of their office, for the substance of the poor—which unjustly they usurp and prodigally they do spend, but principally for the false and deceivable doctrine which is taught and defended by their false prophets, flattering friars, and other such venomous locusts. Which thing, if with single eyes ye do—preferring God's glory and the salvation of your brethren to all worldly commodity, then shall the same God, who solemnly doth pronounce to honor those that do honor him, pour his benediction plentifully upon you; he shall be your buckler, protection, and captain, and shall repress by his strength and wisdom whatsoever Satan by his supposts shall imagine against you.

I am not ignorant that great troubles shall ensue your enterprise. For Satan will not be expelled from the possession of his usurped kingdom without resistance. But if you, as is said, preferring God's glory to your own lives, unfeignedly seek and study to obey his blessed will, then shall your deliverance be such, as evidently it shall be known, that the angels of the eternal do watch, make war, and fight for those that unfeignedly fear the Lord. But if you refuse this, my most reasonable and just petition, what defense that ever you appear to have before men, then shall God, whom in me you contemn, refuse you. He shall pour forth contempt upon you and upon your posterity after you.[57] The spirit of boldness and wisdom shall be taken from you; your enemies shall reign, and you shall die in bondage; yea, God shall cut down the unfruitful trees when they do appear most beautifully to flourish and shall so burn the root that after of you shall neither twig nor branch again spring to glory.[58]

Hereof I need not to adduce unto you examples from the former ages and ancient histories. For your brethren, the nobility of England, are a mirror and glass in the which ye may behold God's just punishment. For as they have refused him and his Evangel, which once in mouth they did profess, so hath he refused them and hath taken from them the spirit of wisdom, boldness, and of counsel. They see and feel their own misery, and yet they have no grace to avoid it. They hate the bondage of strangers, the pride of priests, and the monstriferous empire of a wicked woman, and yet are they compelled to bow their necks to the yoke of the devil, to obey whatsoever the proud Spaniards and wicked Jezebel list to command, and finally to stand with cap in hand till the servants of Satan, the shaven sort, call them to council. This fruit do they reap and gather of their former rebellion and unfaithfulness towards God. They are left confused in their own counsels. He, whom in his members for the pleasure of a wicked woman they have exiled, persecuted, and blasphemed, doth now laugh them to scorn, suffereth them to be penned in bondage of most wicked men, and finally shall adjudge them to the fire everlasting, except that speedily and openly they repent their horrible treason which against God, against his son Christ Jesus, and against the liberty of their own native realm they have committed.[59]

The same plague shall fall upon you, be you assured, if ye refuse the defense of his servants that call for your support. My words are sharp; but consider, my lords, that they are not mine, but that they are the threatenings of the Omnipotent, who assuredly will perform the voices of his prophets how that ever carnal men despise his admonitions. The sword of God's wrath is already drawn which, of necessity, must needs strike when grace offered is obstinately refused.[60]

You have been long in bondage of the devil; blindness, error, and idolatry prevailing against the simple truth of God in that your realm in which God hath made you princes and rulers. But now doth God of his great mercy call you to repentance before he pour forth the uttermost of his vengeance; he crieth to your ears that your religion is nothing but idolatry; he accuseth you of the blood of his saints, which hath been shed by your permission, assistance, and powers. For the tyranny of those raging beasts should have no force, if by your strength they were not maintained. Of those horrible crimes doth now God accuse you, not of purpose to condemn you, but mercifully to absolve and pardon you, as sometime he did those whom Peter accused to have killed the son of God, so that ye be not of mind nor purpose to justify your former iniquity.[61]

Iniquity I call not only the crimes and offenses which have been and yet remain in your manners and lives; but that also which appeareth before men most holy, with hazard of my life, I offer to prove abomination before God, that is, your whole religion to be so corrupt and vain that no true servant of God can communicate with it, because that in so doing, he should manifestly deny Christ Jesus and his eternal verity. I know that your bishops, accompanied with the swarm of the papistical vermin, shall cry, "a damned heretic ought not to be heard." But remember, my lords, what in the beginning I have protested, upon which ground I continually stand, to wit, that I am no heretic nor deceivable teacher, but the servant of Christ Jesus, a preacher of his infallible verity, innocent in all that they can lay to my charge concerning my doctrine, and that therefore by them, being enemies to Christ, I am injustly damned.

From which cruel sentence I have appealed and do appeal, as before mention is made; in the meantime most humbly requiring your honors to take me in your protection, to be auditors of my just defenses, granting unto me the same liberty which Ahab, a wicked King, and Israel, at that a blinded people, granted to Elijah in the like case, that is, that your bishops and the whole rabble of your clergy may be called before you and before the people whom they have deceived, that I be not condemned by multitude, by custom, by authority or law devised by man, but that God himself may be judge betwixt me and my adversaries.[62] Let God, I say, speak by his law, by his Prophets, by Christ Jesus or by his Apostles, and so let him pronounce what religion he approveth; and then, be my enemies never so many and appear they never so strong and so learned, no more do I fear victory than did Elijah, being but one man against the multitude of Baal's priests.

And if they think to have advantage by their councils and doctors, this I further offer: to admit the one and the other as witnesses in all matters debatable, three things—which justly cannot be denied—being granted unto me. First, that the most ancient councils, nighest to the primitive church, in which the learned and godly fathers did examine all matters by God's word, may be holden of most authority. Secondarily, that no determination of council nor man be admitted against the plain verity of God's word nor against the determination of those four chief councils whose authority hath been and is holden by them equal with the authority of the four Evangelists. And last, that no doctor be given greater authority than Augustine requireth to be given to his writings, to wit, if he plainly prove not his affirmation by God's infallible word, that then his sentence be rejected and imputed to the error of man.[63] These things granted and admitted, I shall no more refuse the testimonies of councils and doctors than shall my adversaries.

But and if they will justify those councils which maintain their pride and usurped authority and will reject those which plainly have condemned all such tyranny, negligence, and wicked life, as bishops now do use, and if further they will snatch a doubtful sentence of a doctor and refuse his mind when he speaketh plainly, then will I say that all man is a liar, that credit ought not to be given to an unconstant witness, and that no council ought to prevail nor be admitted against the sentence which God hath pronounced.

And thus, my lords, in few words to conclude: I have offered unto you what God requireth of you, being placed above his people as rulers and princes; I have offered unto you and to the inhabitants of the realm the verity of Christ Jesus; and with the hazard of my life I presently offer to prove the religion which amongst you is maintained by fire and sword to be false, damnable, and diabolical. Which things if ye refuse, defending tyrants in their tyranny, then dare I not flatter; but as it was commanded to Ezekiel boldly to proclaim, so must I cry to you that "you shall perish in your iniquity," that the Lord Jesus shall refuse so many of you as maliciously withstand his eternal verity, and in the days of his apparition, when all flesh shall appear before him, that he shall repel you from his company and shall command you to the fire which never shall be quenched; and then neither shall the multitude be able to resist neither yet the counsels of man be able to prevail against that sentence which he shall pronounce.[64]

God, the father of our Lord Jesus Christ, by the power of his Holy Spirit, so rule and dispose your hearts that with simplicity ye may consider the things that be offered, and that ye may take such order in the same as God in you may be glorified and Christ's flock by you may be edified and comforted to the praise and glory of our Lord Jesus Christ, whose omnipotent spirit rule your hearts in his true fear to the end.

Amen.

Notes

1. [express]
2. Acts 4:12.
3. Heb. 10:10.
4. 1 Cor. 4; Matt. 25.
5. John 3; Rom. 5; Rom. 8; 2 Cor. 5; Rom. 6; Eph. 2, 4, 5.
6. Matt. 10:33.
7. [Unable to burn Knox, who was in Geneva, the ecclesiastical authorities publicly burned his effigy to symbolize their sentence against him.]

8. Deut. 17.
9. Jer. 26.
10. Deut. 17.
11. Jer. 1; Deut. 1, 10, 17. [The quotation is in Jer. 26:14.]
12. Jer. 38. [The quotation is in Jer. 37:20.]
13. [act, deed]
14. Acts 22, 23, 24, 25.
15. Acts 25:9, 10, 11.
16. Jer. 2:8, 13.
17. Isa. 56; Acts 3, 4; 2 Tim. 4; Jude 1; 2 Pet. 2.
18. Rom. 13:1, 2, 3, 4.
19. Rom. 13:6.
20. Isa. 1:23.
21. Jer. 23, 27; Ezek. 13; Hos. 4.
22. Exod. 21, 24, 25.
23. Exod. 28, 29.
24. 2 Chron. 14, 17.
25. 2 Chron. 29:5–11.
26. 2 Chron. 30:6, 7, 8.
27. 2 Chron. 34.
28. 2 Kings 23.
29. 2 Chron. 32.
30. Augustine *Letters* clxxxv.
31. Isa. 49:23.
32. Jer. 38.
33. Jer. 39:16; Jer. 38:9.
34. Deut. 12.
35. Deut. 13:6, 7, 8, 9.
36. 1 Sam. 3, 9, 15, 16.
37. 1 Kings 22.
38. 1 Kings 21.
39. 2 Kings 8.
40. 2 Chron. 15:13.
41. Deut. 13:12–17.
42. Deut. 7, 13, 28, 30.
43. Ezek. 8:12; 9:4.
44. Eph. 2.
45. 1 Sam. 15.
46. Exod. 34:12–16.
47. Exod. 32:20, 21.
48. 1 Kings 2:27.
49. 1 Tim. 3.
50. Matt. 17; Acts 4, 5; 1 Pet. 2:13, 14.
51. Rom. 13:1.
52. Chrysostom *The Epistle to the Romans* 23.
53. *Decretum Gratiani,* quaest. iii, dist. 9.
54. *Decretum Gratiani,* dist. 19.
55. *Decretum Gratiani,* Liber 2, 7, *(de translatione episcopi)* 2.
56. *Decretum Gratiani,* dist. 40.
57. Deut. 28; Lev. 26.
58. Isa. 27, 30.

59. [The suggested parallel was the queen regent's employment of French advisors and officers to assure Scotland's support of French policy.]

60. Let England and Scotland both advert.

61. Acts 2.

62. 1 Kings 18.

63. Augustine *Retractions*, Prologue.

64. Ezek. 33; Dan. 12; Matt. 24, 25, 26.

4

Letter to the Commonalty of Scotland
(1558)

To his beloved brethren, the commonalty of Scotland, John Knox
wisheth grace, mercy, and peace with the spirit of righteous judgment.

What I have required of the Queen Regent, estates, and nobility
as of the chief heads, for this present, of the realm, I cannot cease
to require of you, dearly beloved brethren, which be the commonalty of the same: to wit, that it (notwithstanding that false and
cruel sentence which your disguised bishops have pronounced
against me) would please you to be so favorable unto me as to be
indifferent auditors of my just purgation. Which to do, if God
earnestly move your hearts, as I nothing doubt but that your
enterprise shall redound to the praise of his holy name, so am I
assured that ye and your posterity shall by that means receive most
singular comfort, edification, and profit. For when ye shall hear
the matter debated, ye shall easily perceive and understand upon
what ground and foundation is builded that religion which
amongst you is this day defended by fire and sword. As for my
own conscience, I am most assuredly persuaded that whatsoever is
used in the papistical church is altogether repugning to Christ's
blessed ordinance and is nothing but mortal venom, of which
whosoever drinketh, I am assuredly persuaded, that therewith he
drinketh death and damnation, except by true conversion unto
God he be purged from the same. But because that long silence of
God's word hath begotten ignorance almost in all sorts of man,
and ignorance joined with long custom hath confirmed supersti-

tion in the hearts of many, I therefore in the name of the Lord Jesus desire audience as well of you the commonalty, my brethren, as of the estates and nobility of the realm that in public preaching I may have place amongst you at large to utter my mind in all matters of controversy this day in religion. And further I desire that ye, concurring with your nobility, would compel your bishops and clergy to cease their tyranny; and also, that for the better assurance and instruction of your conscience, ye would compel your said bishops and false teachers to answer by the Scriptures of God to such objections and crimes as shall be laid against their vain religion, false doctrine, wicked life, and slanderous conversation.

Here I know that it shall be objected that I require of you a thing most unreasonable: to wit, that ye should call your religion in doubt, which hath been approved and established by so long continuance and by the consent of so many men before you. But I shortly answer that neither is the long process of time, neither yet the multitude of men a sufficient approbation which God will allow for our religion. For as some of the most ancient writers do witness, neither can long process of time justify an error, neither can the multitude of such as follow it change the nature of the same.[1] But if it was an error in the beginning, so is it in the end; and the longer that it be followed and the more that do receive it, it is the more pestilent and more to be avoided. For if antiquity or multitude of men could justify any religion, then was the idolatry of the gentiles and now is the abomination of the Turks good religion. For antiquity approved the one, and a multitude hath received and doth defend the other.

But otherwise to answer, godly men may wonder from what fountain such a sentence doth flow that no man ought to try his faith and religion by God's word, but that he may safely believe and follow everything which antiquity and a multitude have approved. The Spirit of God doth otherwise teach us. For the wisdom of God, Christ Jesus himself remitted his adversaries to Moses and the Scriptures to try by them whether his doctrine was of God or not.[2] The Apostles Paul and Peter command men to try the religion which they profess by God's plain Scriptures and do praise men for so doing.[3] St. John straitly commandeth that we believe not every spirit, but willeth us to try the spirits whether they be of God or not.[4] Now seeing that these evident testimonies of the Holy Ghost will us to try our faith and religion by the plain word of God, wonder it is that the papists will not be content that their religion and doctrine come under the trial of the same.

If this sentence of Christ be true (as it is most true, seeing it springeth from the verity itself), "who so evil doeth, hateth the light, neither will he come to the light lest that his evil works be manifested and rebuked," then do our papists by their own sentence condemn themselves and their religion.[5] For insofar as they refuse examination and trial, they declare that they know some fault which the light will utter; which is a cause of their fear and why they claim to that privilege that no man dispute of their religion. The verity and truth, being of the nature of fine, purified gold, doth not fear the trial of the furnace, but the stubble and chaff of man's inventions—such is their religion—may not abide the flame of the fire.

True it is that Mahomet pronounced this sentence, that no man should in pain of death dispute or reason of the ground of his religion. Which law to this day, by the art of Satan, is yet observed amongst the Turks to their mortal blindness and horrible blaspheming of Christ Jesus and of his true religion. And from Mahomet (or rather from Satan, father of all lies) hath the pope and his rabble learned this former lesson; to wit, that their religion should not be disputed upon, but what the fathers have believed that ought and must the children approve. And in so devising, Satan lacked not his foresight. For no one thing hath more established the kingdom of that Roman Antichrist than this most wicked decree: to wit, that no man was permitted to reason of his power or to call his laws in doubt. This thing is most assured: that whensoever the papistical religion shall come to examination, it shall be found to have no other ground than hath the religion of Mahomet, to wit, man's invention, devise, and dreams, overshadowed with some color of God's word.

And therefore, brethren, seeing that the religion is as the stomach to the body, which if it be corrupted, doth infect the whole members, it is necessary that the same be examined; and if it be found replenished with pestilent humors (I mean with fantasies of men), then of necessity it is that those be purged, else shall your bodies and souls perish forever. For of this I would ye were most certainly persuaded: that a corrupt religion defileth the whole life of man, appear it never so holy.

Neither would I that ye should esteem the reformation and care of religion less to appertain to you because ye are no kings, rulers, judges, nobles, nor in authority. Beloved brethren, ye are God's creatures, created and formed to his own image and similitude, for whose redemption was shed the most precious blood of the only beloved son of God, to whom he hath commanded his Gospel and glad-tidings to be preached, and for whom he hath prepared the heavenly inheritance, so that ye will not obstinately refuse and disdainfully contemn the means which he hath appointed to obtain the same, to wit, his blessed Evangel, which now he offereth unto you to the end that ye may be saved. For the Gospel and glad-tidings of the kingdom truly preached, is the power of God to the salvation of every believer, which to credit and receive, you, the commonalty, are no less addebted than be your rulers and princes.[6]

For albeit God hath put and ordained distinction and difference betwixt king and subjects, betwixt the rulers and the common people in the regiment and administration of civil policies, yet in the hope of the life to come he hath made all equal.[7] For as in Christ Jesus the Jew hath no greater prerogative than hath the gentile, and man than hath the woman, the learned than the un-learned, the lord than the servant, but all are one in him, so is there but one way and means to attain to the participation of his benefits and spiritual graces, which is a lively faith working by charity. And therefore I say that it doth no less appertain to you, beloved breth-ren, to be assured that your faith and religion be grounded and established upon the true and undoubted word of God than to your princes or rulers. For as your bodies cannot escape corporal death, if with your princes ye eat or drink deadly poison (although it be by ignorance or negligence), so shall ye not escape the death everlasting, if with them ye profess a corrupt religion.

Yea, except in heart ye believe and with mouth ye confess the Lord Jesus to be the only savior of the world—which ye cannot do, except ye embrace his Evangel offered, ye cannot escape death and damnation.[8] For as the just liveth by his own faith, so doth the unfaithful perish by his infidelity. And as true faith is engendered, nourished, and maintained in the hearts of God's elect by Christ's Evangel truly preached, so is infidelity and unbelief fostered by concealing and repressing the same. And thus, if ye look for the life everlasting, ye must try if ye stand in faith; and if ye would be assured of a true and lively faith, ye must needs have Christ Jesus truly preached unto you. And this is the cause, dear brethren, that so oft I repeat and so constantly I affirm that to you it doth no less appertain than to your kings or princes to provide that Christ Jesus be truly preached amongst you, seeing that without his true knowledge can neither of you both attain to salvation. And this is the point wherein I say all man is equal: "That as all be descended from Adam, by whose sin and inobedience did death enter into the world, so it behooved all that shall obtain life to be ingrafted in one, that is, in the Lord Jesus, who, being the just servant, doth by his knowledge justify many," to wit, all that unfeignedly believe in him.[9]

Of this equality (and that God requireth no less of the subject, be he never so poor, than of the prince and rich man in matters of religion), he hath given an evident declaration in the law of Moses. For when the tabernacle was builded, erected, and set in order, God did provide how it and the things appertaining to the same should be sustained, so that they should not fall in decay. And this provision, albeit heaven and earth obey his empire, would he not take from the secret and hid treasures which lie dispersed in the veins of the earth, neither yet would he take it from the rich and potent of his people; but he did command that every man of the sons of Israel, were he rich or were he poor, that came in compt from twenty years and upward should yearly pay half a sicle[10] for an oblation to the Lord, in the remembrance of their redemption, and for an expiation or cleansing to their souls; which money God commanded should be bestowed upon the ornaments and necessaries of the tabernacle of testimony.[11]

He furthermore added a precept that the rich should give no more for that use and in that behalf than should the poor, neither yet that the poor should give any less than should the rich in that consideration. This law, to man's reason and judgment, may appear very unreasonable, for some rich man might have given a thousand sicles with less hurt of his substance than some poor man might have paid the half sicle. And yet God maketh all equal and will that the one shall pay no more than the other, neither yet the poor any less than the rich. This law, I say, may appear very unequal. But if the cause which God addeth be observed, we shall find in the same the great mercy and inestimable wisdom of God to appear; which cause is expressed in these words: "This money received from the children of Israel thou shalt give in the service of the tabernacle that it may be to the children of Israel for a remembrance before the Lord, that he may be merciful to your souls."[12]

This cause, I say, doth evidently declare that, as the whole multitude was delivered from the bondage of Egypt by the mighty power of God alone, so was every member of the same, without respect of person, sanctified by his grace, the rich in that behalf nothing preferred to the poorest. For by no merit nor worthiness of man was he moved to choose and to establish his habitation and dwelling amongst them. But their felicity, prerogative, and honor, which they had above all other nations, proceeded only from the fountain of his eternal goodness, who loved them freely, as that he freely had chosen them to be his priestly kingdom and holy people from all nations of the earth. Thus to honor them, that he would dwell in the midst of them, he neither was moved, I say, by the wisdom of the wise, by the riches of the potent, neither yet by the virtue and holiness of any estate amongst them; but of mere goodness did he love them, and with his presence did he honor that whole people. And therefore, to paint out the same—his common love to the whole multitude—and to cut off occasions of contention and doubts of conscience, he would receive no more from the rich than from the poor for the maintenance of that his tabernacle, by the which was represented his presence amongst them.[13]

If the rich had been preferred to the poor, then, as the one should have been puffed up with pride, as that he had been more acceptable to God by reason of his greater gift, so should the conscience of the other have been troubled and wounded, thinking that his poverty was an impediment that he could not stand in so perfect favor with God as did the other, because he was not able to give so much as did the rich to the maintenance of his tabernacle. But he, who of mercy, as said is, did choose his habitation amongst them and also that best knoweth what lieth within man, did provide the remedy for the one and for the other, making them equal in that behalf who in other things were most unequal. If the poor should have found himself grieved by reason of that tax and that as much was imposed upon him as upon the rich, yet had he no small cause of joy that God himself would please to compare him and to make him equal in the maintenance of his tabernacle to the most rich and potent in Israel.

If this equality was commanded by God for maintenance of that transitory tabernacle, which was but a shadow of a better to come, is not the same required of us, who now hath the verity which is Christ Jesus, who, being clad with our nature is made Immanuel, that is, God with us?[14] "Whose natural body, albeit it be received in the heavens where he must abide till all be complete that is forespoken by the Prophets, yet hath he promised to be present with us to the end of the world."[15] And for that purpose and for the more assurance of his promise, he hath erected amongst us here in earth the signs of his own presence with us, his spiritual tabernacle, the true preaching of his word, and right administrations of his sacraments, to the maintenance whereof is no less bound the subject than the prince, the poor than the rich. For as the price which was given for man's redemption is one, so requireth God of all that shall be partakers of the benefits of the same a like duty which is a plain confession that by Christ Jesus alone we have received whatsoever was lost in Adam. Of the prince doth God require that he refuse himself and that he follow Christ Jesus; of the subject he requireth the same. Of the kings and judges it is required that they kiss the son, that is, give honor, subjection, and obedience to him; and from such reverence doth not God exempt the subject that shall be saved. And this is that equality which is betwixt the kings and subjects, the most rich or noble, and betwixt the poorest and men of lowest estate: to wit, that as the one is obliged to believe in heart and with mouth confess the Lord Jesus to be the only savior of the world, so also is the other. Neither is there any of God's children—who hath attained to the years of discretion—so poor but that he hath thus much to bestow upon the ornaments and maintenance of their spiritual tabernacle; neither yet is there any so rich of whose hand God requireth any more.

For albeit that David gathered great substance for the building of the temple, that Solomon with earnest diligence and incredible expenses erected and finished the same, that Hezekiah and Josiah purged the religion which before was corrupted, yet to them was God no further debtor in that respect than he was to the most simple of the faithful posterity of faithful Abraham.[16] For their diligence, zeal, and works gave rather testimony and confession before men what honor they did bear to God, what love to his word, and reverence to his religion than that any work proceeding from them did either establish or yet increase God's favor towards them, who freely did love them in Christ his son before the foundation of the world was laid. So that these forenamed by their notable works gave testimony of their unfeigned faith, and the same doth the poorest that unfeignedly and openly professeth Christ Jesus, that doth embrace his glad-tidings offered, that doth abhor superstition, and fly from idolatry. The poorest, I say, and most simple that this day in earth, in the days of this cruel persecution, firmly believeth in Christ and boldly doth confess him before this wicked generation is no less acceptable before God, neither is judged in his presence to have done any less in promoting Christ his cause, than is the king that by the sword and power which he hath received of God rooteth out idolatry and so advanceth Christ's glory. But to return to our former purpose, it is no less required, I say, of the subject to believe in Christ and to profess his true religion than of the prince and king. And therefore I affirm that in God's presence it shall not excuse you to allege that ye were no chief rulers and therefore that the care and reformation of religion did not appertain unto you.

Ye, dear brethren, as before is said, are the creatures of God, created to his own image and similitude, to whom it is commanded to hear the voice of your heavenly father, to embrace his son Christ Jesus, to fly from all doctrine and religion which he hath not approved by his own will revealed to us in his most blessed word.[17] To which precepts and charges if ye be found inobedient, ye shall perish in your iniquity as rebels and stubborn servants that have no pleasure to obey the good will of their sovereign Lord, who most lovingly doth call for your obedience. And therefore, brethren, in this behalf it is your part to be careful and diligent. For the question is not of things temporal which, although they be endangered, yet by diligence and process of time may after be redressed; but it is of the damnation of your bodies and souls and of the loss of the life everlasting, which once lost can never be recovered. And therefore I say that it behooveth you to be careful and diligent in this so weighty a matter, lest that ye, contemning this occasion which God now offereth, find not the like, although that after with groaning and sobs ye languish for the same.

And that ye be not ignorant of what occasion I mean, in few words I shall express it. Not only I, but with me also divers other godly and learned men, do offer unto you our labors faithfully to instruct you in the ways of the eternal our God and in the sincerity of Christ's Evangel, which this day by the pestilent generation of Antichrist (I mean by the pope and by his most ungodly clergy) are almost hid from the eyes of men. We offer to jeopard our lives for the salvation of your souls, and by manifest Scriptures to prove that religion, which amongst you is maintained by fire and sword, to be vain, false, and diabolical. We require nothing of you but that patiently ye will hear our doctrine, which is not ours but is the doctrine of salvation revealed to the world by the only son of God, and that ye will examine our reasons, by the which we offer to prove the papistical religion to be abominable before God. And last we require that by your powers the tyranny of those cruel beasts (I mean of priests and friars) may be bridled till we have uttered our minds in all matters this day debatable in religion. If these things, in the fear of God, ye grant to me and unto others that unfeignedly for your salvation and for God's glory require the same, I am assured that of God ye shall be blessed, whatsoever Satan shall devise against you. But and if ye contemn or refuse God who thus lovingly offereth unto you salvation and life, ye shall neither escape plagues temporal, which shortly shall apprehend you, neither yet the torment prepared for the devil and for his angels, except by speedy repentance ye return to the Lord, whom now ye refuse, if that ye refuse the messengers of his word.

But yet I think ye doubt what ye ought and may do in this so weighty a matter. In few words I will declare my conscience in the one and in the other. Ye ought to prefer the glory of God, the promoting of Christ his Evangel, and the salvation of your souls to all thing that be in earth; and ye, although ye be but subjects, may lawfully require of your superiors—be it of your king, be it of your lords, rulers, and powers—that they provide for you true preachers and that they expel such, as under the names of pastors, devour and destroy the flock, not feeding the same, as Christ Jesus hath commanded. And if in this point your superiors be negligent or yet pretend to maintain tyrants in their tyranny, most justly ye may provide true teachers for yourselves, be it in your cities, towns, or villages; them ye may maintain and defend against all that shall persecute them and by that means shall labor to defraud you of that most comfortable food of your souls, Christ's Evangel truly preached. Ye may, moreover, withhold the fruits and profits which your false bishops and clergy most injustly receive of you unto such time as they be compelled faithfully to do their charge and duties which is to preach unto Christ Jesus truly, rightly to minister his sacraments according to his own institution, and so to watch for the salvation of your souls, as is commanded by Christ Jesus himself and by his Apostles Paul and Peter.[18]

If God shall move your hearts in his true fear to begin to practice these things and to demand and crave the same of your superiors, which most lawfully ye may do, then I doubt not, but of his great mercy and free grace, he shall illuminate the eyes of your minds that his undoubted verity shall be a lantern to your feet to guide and lead you in all the ways which his godly wisdom doth approve. He shall make your enemies tremble before your faces; he shall establish his blessed Evangel amongst you to the salvation and perpetual comfort of yourselves and of your posterity after.

But and if, as God forbid, the love of friends, the fear of princes, and the wisdom of the world draw you back from God and from his son Christ Jesus, be ye certainly persuaded that ye shall drink the cup of his vengeance—so many, I mean, as shall contemn and despise this loving call of your heavenly father. It will not excuse you, dear brethren, in the presence of God, neither yet will it avail you in the day of his visitation, to say, "we were but simple subjects; we could not redress the fault and crimes of our rulers, bishops, and clergy; we called for reformation and wished for the same, but lords' brethren were bishops, their sons were abbots, and the friends of great men had the possession of the church; and so we were compelled to give obedience to all that they demanded." These vain excuses, I say, will nothing avail you in the presence of God who requireth no less of the subjects than of the rulers: that they decline from evil, and that they do good, that they abstain from idolatry, superstition, blasphemy, murder, and other such horrible crimes, which his law forbiddeth and yet not the less are openly committed and maliciously defended in that miserable realm.

And if ye think that ye are innocent because ye are not the chief authors of such iniquity, ye are utterly deceived. For God doth not only punish the chief offenders, but with them doth he damn the consenters to iniquity; and all are judged to consent that, knowing impiety committed, give no testimony that the same displeaseth them.[19] To speak this matter more plain, as your princes and rulers are criminal with your bishops of all idolatry committed, and of all innocent blood that is shed for the testimony of Christ's truth, and that because they maintain them in their tyranny, so are you—I mean so many of you as give no plain confession to the contrary— criminals and guilty with your princes and rulers of the same crimes, because ye assist and maintain your princes in their blind rage and give no declaration that their tyranny displeaseth you.

This doctrine, I know, is strange to the blind world, but the verity of it hath been declared in all notable punishments from the beginning. When the original world perished by water, when Sodom and Gomorrah were consumed by fire, and finally when Jerusalem was horribly destroyed, doth any man think that all were alike wicked before the world?[20] Evident it is that they were not, if they shall be judged according to their external facts. For some were young and could not be oppressors, neither yet defile themselves with unnatural and beastly lusts; some were pitiful and gentle of nature and did not thirst for the blood of Christ nor of his Apostles. But did any escape the plagues and vengeance which did apprehend the multitude? Let the Scriptures witness and the histories be considered which plainly do testify that by the waters all flesh in earth at that time did perish (Noah and his family reserved), that none escaped in Sodom and in the other cities adjacent, except Lot and his two daughters. And evident it is that in that famous city Jerusalem, in that last and horrible destruction of the same, none escaped God's vengeance, except so many as before were dispersed.

And what is the cause of this severity, seeing that all were not alike offenders? Let flesh cease to dispute with God, and let all man by these examples learn betimes to fly and avoid the society and company of the proud contemners of God, if that they list not to be partakers of their plagues. The cause is evident, if we can be subject, without grudging, to God's judgments which in themselves are most holy and just. For in the original world none was found that either did resist tyranny and oppression that universally was used, either yet that earnestly reprehended the same. In Sodom was none found that did againststand that furious and beastly multitude that did compass about and besiege the house of Lot. None would believe Lot that the city should be destroyed. And finally, in Jerusalem was none found that studied to repress the tyranny of the priests who were conjured against Christ and his Evangel; but all fainted (I except ever such as gave witness with their blood or their flying that such impiety displeased them), all kept silence, by the which all approved iniquity and joined hands with the tyrants; and so were all arrayed and set, as it had been, in one battle against the omnipotent and against his son Christ Jesus. For whosoever gathereth not with Christ in the day of his harvest, is judged to scatter. And therefore of one vengeance temporal were they all partakers.

Which thing, as before I have touched, ought to move you to the deep consideration of your duties in these last and most perilous times. The iniquity of your bishops is more than manifest: their filthy lives infect the air; the innocent blood which they shed crieth vengeance in the ears of our God; the idolatry and abomination, which openly they commit and without punishment maintain, doth corrupt and defile the whole land; and none amongst you doth unfeignedly study for any redress of such enormities. Will God in this behalf hold you as innocents? Be not deceived, dear brethren. God hath punished not only the proud tyrants, filthy persons, and cruel murderers, but also such as with them draw the yoke of iniquity, was it by flattering their offenses, obeying their injust commandments, or in winking at their manifest iniquity. All such, I say, hath God once punished with the chief offenders. Be ye assured, brethren, that as he is immutable of nature, so will he not pardon in you that which severely he hath punished in others, and now the less, because he hath plainly admonished you of the dangers to come and hath offered you his mercy before he pour forth his wrath and displeasure upon the inobedient.

God, the father of our Lord Jesus Christ, who is father of glory and God of all consolation, give you the spirit of wisdom and open unto you the knowledge of himself by the means of his dear son, by the which ye may attain to the esperance and hope that, after the troubles of this transitorious life, ye may be partakers of the riches of that glorious inheritance which is prepared for such as refuse themselves and fight under the banner of Christ Jesus in the day of this his battle; that in deep consideration of the same, ye may learn to prefer the invisible and eternal joys to the vain pleasures that are present. God further grant you his Holy Spirit, righteously to consider what I in his name have required of your nobility and of you the subjects, and move you all together so to answer that my petition be not a testimony of your just condemnation when the Lord Jesus shall appear to revenge the blood of his saints and the contempt of his most holy word. Amen.

Sleep not in sin, for vengeance is prepared against all inobedient. Fly from Babylon, if ye will not be partakers of her plagues.

Be witness to my appellation. Grace be with you. From Geneva, the 14 of July, 1558.

Your brother to command in godliness,
John Knox.

Notes

1. Cyprian *To Demetrian;* Lactantius *The Divine Institutes* ii; Tertullian, *Apology.*
2. John 5, 7.
3. Acts 17; 2 Pet. 1.
4. 1 John 4.
5. John 3:20.
6. Rom. 1.
7. Gal. 3.
8. Hab. 2; Mark 16; John 3.
9. Isa. 53; John 3, 5; Rom. 5:12–15.
10. [shekel]
11. Exod. 30.
12. Exod. 30:16.
13. Exod. 30.
14. Heb. 9.
15. Isa. 8; Matt. 28; Acts 3:21.
16. 1 Chron. 29; 2 Chron. 3, 4, 5, 29, 30, 35.
17. Matt. 17.
18. John 21; Acts 20.
19. Rom. 1.
20. Gen. 7, 19; Flavius Josephus *Antiquities of the Jews* xx.8.5; Hegisippus [Eusebius *Ecclesiastical History* iii.5.]

5
The Second Blast (1558)[1]

Because many are offended at *The First Blast of the Trumpet*, in which I affirm that to promote a woman to bear rule or empire above any realm, nation, or city is repugnant to nature, contumely to God, and a thing most contrarious to his revealed and approved ordinance, and because also that some hath promised—as I understand—a confutation of the same, I have delayed *The Second Blast* till such time as their reasons appear, by the which I either may be reformed in opinion or else shall have further occasion more simply and plainly to utter my judgment. Yet in the meantime, for the discharge of my conscience, and for avoiding suspicion which might be engendered by reason of my silence, I could not cease to notify these subsequent propositions which, by God's grace, I purpose to entreat in *The Second Blast* promised.

1. It is not birth only nor propinquity of blood that maketh a king lawfully to reign above a people, professing Christ Jesus and his eternal verity, but in his election must the ordinance which God hath established in the election of inferior judges be observed.

2. No manifest idolater nor notorious transgressor of God's holy precepts ought to be promoted to any public regiment, honor, or dignity in any realm, province, or city that hath subjected the self to Christ Jesus and his blessed Evangel.

3. Neither can oath nor promise bind any such people to obey and maintain tyrants against God and against his truth known.

4. But, if either rashly they have promoted any manifest wicked person, or yet ignorantly have chosen such a one as after declareth himself unworthy of regiment above the people of God—and such

be all idolaters and cruel persecutors, most justly may the same men depose and punish him that unadvisedly before they did nominate, appoint, and elect.

"If the eye be single, the whole body shall be clear."[2]

Notes

1. [This was published in July 1558, in the same volume with *Appellation* and *Letter to the Commonalty*.]

2. Matt. 6:22.